PRAISE FOR *F*

From Fear to Faith is a journey from fear and sham ... ual ... ure and the God behind it. W ... m- pelling stories from a numb... ... ... :his journey. They give voice to a growing phenomenon in conservative Christian culture of disenchantment with conventional and apologetically driven answers to difficult and pressing questions posed by Scripture, modern culture, and the intersection of the two. The stories in this volume will be an encouragement to those struggling with their own transition from familiar yet dissonant surroundings to unexplored but inviting spiritual and intellectual territory. The broader vision of the volume is a call to build cultures of trust, where Christians can feel that they will be honored and valued for taking the risk to ask honest questions rather than being dismissed, marginalized, or ostracized. Too many are growing dissatisfied with the status quo, and are looking for language to move on. This volume will help them on their way.

Peter Enns, Ph.D, Biblical Studies, Eastern University

This book offers many variant forms of the story of discovering the force of the Gospel that lies behind the illusions and distortions of fundamentalism. The authors witness to an emancipation when the old, phony "protections" are abandoned. Coming to such an awareness cannot be hurried or coerced, but it is an urgent enterprise. As one author concludes, "I needed to grow up."

Dr. Walter Brueggemann, Columbia Theological Seminary

Many strange things are said and done in the name of Jesus of Nazareth. Many of them are alien to the Christian gospel, even though they are done in the gospel's name. Many of them are toxic, destructive both of persons and societies. They march under the banner of Christian fundamentalism.

This interesting and important book is the chronicle of spiritual journeys that persons have taken from the prisons of fundamentalism [characterized by biblical literalism, anti-science, fear rather than love as the basis of our relationship with God] to the world of catholic (small c), ecumenical churches. For these persons, it has been a journey from slavery in Egypt to freedom in the Promised Land.

The persons whose stories this book tells, are now living in what they believe to be mature communities of faith, where they are growing spiritually and finding the vocations to which they believe God is calling them. Several of them have been called to the formal ministries of their churches and have been ordained. Others have found joy and peace living out their discipleship as lay persons. This important book is their story.

William Boyd Grove, Bishop (retired)
The United Methodist Church

Every once in a while, you are gifted with a growing realization that the book you are reading has needed to be written for a very long time. *From Fear to Faith* is a book like that. In the vulnerable, sometimes excruciating details of a journey into post-fundamentalist faith, we the readers are invited to feel the depth, integrity, and passions given to some of us whose paths began in places we could never have imagined, if they hadn't been willing to offer them for us, without judgment, blame, or condemnation. Whether beginning in inherited, sectarian beliefs or an avowed atheism of humane reaction, these authors demonstrate the depth of their own inner work so that all who are willing can hold the fears together, in peace. Authors and readers alike may see the way to move through fear into faith with clarity and compassion, toward a better world for us all. We have needed this book for a very long time.

Lisa M. Hess, PhD, Associate Professor of Practical Theology
and Contextual Ministries,
United Theological Seminary, Dayton, OH

These essays revive the ancient tradition of testimony – but in a surprising and compelling direction. The authors recount their journeys from intellectually and spiritually restrictive expressions of Christianity to a vibrant and satisfying faith. Readers will grieve the authors' painful moments and celebrate their joy. The stories testify that we need not fear doubt, for doubt often opens the path to joy and fulfillment.

Greg Carey, PhD, Professor of New Testament
Lancaster Theological Seminary, Lancaster, PA

From Fear to Faith

Joel Watts & Travis Milam, editors

Energion Publications
Gonzalez, Florida
2013

ISBN10: 1-938434-60-9
ISBN13: 978-1-938434-60-0
Library of Congress Control Number: 2013939541

Energion Publications
P. O. Box 841
Gonzalez, FL 32560

energionpubs.com
pubs@energion.com
850-525-3916

ACKNOWLEDGMENTS

The editors of this volume would like to thank the contributors who decided to put themselves out there. They have taken a chance with publishing in this volume, and any success is due them. We would also like to thank our publisher who has worked with us even when we missed so many deadlines we just stopped setting them.

Joel would like to thank his wife and his children for forgiving him for the years spent in fear and for loving him as he made the transition. He would also like to thank the Pathfinders' Sunday School who has yet to actually vote on renaming the class after him but he has hopes that they will come to their senses and make the right decision sooner rather than later when most Sunday School classes are renamed if you know what he means. They provided him no small amount of encouragement in the darker days, even when he hid them, during the transition. To Tom Burger, who will always be Joel's first anchor to Christ Church United Methodist. To the men's discussion group — to Skid, to Frank, to Bishop Grove and to Charlie ... "it is finally his, Charlie." To the Doctors Flanagan — pastor, deacon, teachers — who never pushed ... too much and who provided the place to think. He would also like to express his thanks to the Publishing Houses — those who bring the books to the bloggers — for giving Joel a chance to review for them. As you'll see, this helped him in unspeakable ways. Joel has a wicked sense of humor and therefore would love to thank all of those in his life who made this book possible, much like they did at the end of the *Fun with Dick and Jane* movie, but he figures that he couldn't get away with this. Finally, Joel would like to thank his blog readers who more than once sent notes of encouragement.

Travis would like to acknowledge all those who have helped make this possible. To God: for reminding him that he does not have to live in fear to be His child. To Jackie, for helping him realize he is capable of great things and for her love and affection. To his boys, for showing him that knowing about God is truly not the same as knowing God. To his parents, for allowing him to think for myself and make his own decisions, even when this meant choosing a different path. To his friend Joel, for having the faith that he could do something such as this when he did not have it himself. To all those along his journey who have helped, prodded, listened, taught, and prayed: thank you and God bless you all.

TABLE OF CONTENTS

INTRODUCTION

Joel L. Watts

This book has come to fruition by the insistence of my wife and wise counseling of Ric Hardison. It is a long time coming.

We are in the middle of something of a resurgence in the United States of conservative churches.[1] There are numerous reasons for this, but the reasons are not so much the focus of this volume. Instead, the focus is something more tangible. This volume focuses on people who have lived in these conservative churches and have moved away from them. These are the stories of the why and the how. Why did they move and how they made it through. Some may laugh or dismiss the transition out of these conservative churches, but it is nothing to laugh at. If it goes wrong, the victim will be as militant an atheist as they were once militant Christians. If the transition is handled sloppily, it may result in severe emotional trauma. This is why they have professionals who help to bring people out of cults. Because it takes time, love, and know-how.

Some of these people were selected to tell their stories because I was familiar with them throughout my years of blogging at unsettledchristianity.com. Others volunteered. All of them are important. All of them, regardless of the outcome, have made it where so many have failed. Do not judge us or pity us, only listen

---

1 Kelley, Dean M. *Why Conservative Churches Are Growing: A Study in Sociology of Religion with a New Preface.* Mercer University Press, 1996.

"Why Conservative Churches Are Growing." *Christian Post*, n.d. http://www.christianpost.com/news/49988/.

to us. We have shared something that is unique, terrible, and ultimately, beautiful.

This is not a book about telling secrets, airing dirty laundry, or otherwise attempting to disparage others. Indeed, I suspect that many of these authors still have family and friends who remain still yet in the places they have come from. This is about warning, pleading, and hoping that more people will come out of sects that use nothing but fear, disguised as liberty, to coerce the human spirit into bondage, not for God, but in too many cases, against God.

The philosophy of this book is simple. These are the stories as lived by the authors. Whether or not they name names or simply stick to the deeply spiritual move, it is up to them. But the accounts are true. Sometimes, even repeated. You will notice a common thread, no doubt, between the stories, and that is in itself a part of the philosophy as well.

There is always a danger in putting oneself out there for the world to read, to disparage, to ridicule, but theirs is the benefit as well — these stories will touch a soul somewhere, to rescue them from fear, to pull them to faith.

I

From Fear to Faith

On a dark night, Kindled in love with yearnings–oh, happy chance!– I went forth without being observed, My house being now at rest.

Travis Milam

My journey began as many others have begun: in church. I grew up going to church, usually Sunday morning, evening and Wednesday evening. Summers were for Vacation Bible School. The Bible was the final say in matters of faith and to say that God had called you to do or be something was the end of an argument. It was clear, simple, and easy. All one had to do was follow the rules, make Jesus Lord of your life and believe the Bible.

I grew up in this culture. I was saved (converted) at the age of seven and baptized. I then knew I was set for life because that was everything that God required of me. Oh, I knew that He wanted me to tell others about Him so they could be saved and that I was to read my Bible and know scripture, but as long as I was saved, I really did not have to worry about other things.

I grew up in a Fundamental, Independent, Baptist church. This meant that aside from the Baptist title, we had no denominational framework. We chose our pastors and pretty much did as we pleased in the community as far as helping and reaching out to others. We had communion, or the Lord's Supper, maybe once a quarter and only on Sunday Evenings. There was no liturgy as that was viewed as High Church and not what Christ had wanted for us. However, if things deviated from the bulletin on Sunday mornings, there were murmurings. Sunday evenings were generally a more casual version of Sunday morning. Wednesday evenings were Bible study and AWANA. Vacation Bible School was usually a guest speaker who came and gave us Bible stories and had us compete with others in sword drills and scripture memorization. Sunday School was learning about the Bible and how we could live as better Christians. There were, and still are, many good people in this church and by many accounts I have heard, we were fairly tame in theology and holding everyone to the "rules." We did help people and there were many who lived the Christian life. However, there was always in the background a feeling that you were never quite good enough and that you had somehow always managed to make God unhappy or angry.

As I grew up and became a part of this church, I took on many traits that have followed me for many years. I learned what was right and wrong and learned good moral values. I learned many scriptures that have remained with me to this day. These, and many others, were positive things that I picked up growing up in this environment. There were however, other aspects that I learned that were not positive nor were they things that I am proud of today.

While I was taught that one was saved by grace and that salvation was eternal, I learned that one could see who was not really walking the walk of a good Christian. I also learned what it took to give the "correct" answers and live the "correct" life. On the outside I exuded confidence and showed I truly lived the good Christian life. On the inside, I was consumed by guilt that I did not pray enough, that I did not read my Bible enough, that I did not love God enough. It was taught that a good Christian did all these things and did them without complaint, that they did them willingly and readily. But even as I was consumed by private guilt, I was also consumed by self righteous pride. I kept my hair short, listened to the "correct" music (anything with a pop or rock beat was suspect, more on that later), wore "church clothes" to services, carried my Bible to church, and did not allow bad language to come from my mouth. In short, I was the perfect youth group member. I did not give my parents a hard time, listened to my elders and never questioned unless my parents had questioned something. I was good and I knew it. I knew that God was proud of me and that He wanted others to be like me. But still, I knew something was not right within me.

The church in which I was raised was rather conservative. Being Fundamental Baptist assured that. We believed the Bible was the WORD OF GOD and to question anything in it was to question God. This was not acceptable. Being a liberal in politics, religion, or socially was seen as close to committing the unpardonable sin. We did not like sin and one had to repent and show that it was a true repentance before being accepted in any social circles. Revivals were, looking back, really week long guilt trips about how we did not do enough for God and how God was going to bring judgment on the world and the nation if things did not change. This environment was natural to me. It was where I felt comfortable. It was safe because I knew the routines and I knew the answers. I liked it because it was easy, certain, and safe. God was in His box that I helped to put Him in and that was just fine with me.

What broke my little bubble was going to a show choir competition at a college. This college was affiliated with the American Baptist Churches USA and I had never heard of that. I believed all Baptists were like me. All the other denominations, especially Roman Catholics and other non-Protestants, were wrong, wrong, wrong and I had no problem with them going to hell. Well, I did, but they had to become like me or my church to really become Christian. In other words, I was the person to whom Paul was speaking in Galatians.

During this time I always had fear and guilt that I was not being a good Christian. My fear was that people would find out that I was not as good a person as thought, and that they would not respect me or think me good any longer. My guilt was that I always believed I was failing God and not doing His will. My teenage years were ones I spent in a perpetual Looking over my shoulder to make sure I was doing right and not doing something with which God would get angry. This explains why I was such a "good" person: it was not really because I wanted to be, it was because I believed that I had to be and I always tried to do what was expected of me.

My journey to the faith I have today began in college. I attended the school where I had encountered a different Baptist from me. It was here that I began a long and hard road to become who I am today.

My first class was Survey Into Biblical Literature. I discovered very quickly that I had no problem with the class as I knew most of it from Sunday School. But there were some "issues." The professor had us purchase a modern English translation for class. I was a King James man. I had no problem with other versions, but I did not want to use them. There were also the new ideas and theories that were taught that I had never heard before. One was the JEPD theory. I had never heard that the Bible might be edited before. To me this was pure heresy. The Bible was inspired and God was the one who gave the inspiration, therefore there were no errors as well as no editing. But then something happened. I began to read, really read, the Bible and discovered that things were not so cut and dried as I had thought. There were parts that could only be explained by editing. I discovered I had never really read the Bible, just did a hit and miss reading, picking up stories here and there and learning what I thought was important. This one class would have an effect upon me that I really would not understand until later in my journey.

Along this journey, I met Dr. Bill Fowler who was the Chaplain of the college as well as my professor for Biblical Lit. He was funny, intelligent, caring and above all a servant of God. He showed me that I could be a good Christian and not follow all the rules I had imposed upon myself or that I believed my church had imposed. Slowly, under his and others influence, the shackles of fear began to loosen. In fact, it was Dr. Fowler who began a campaign to get me into the ministry. Needless to say, things were changing for me.

I began to realize that there were good Christians in all denominations. I slowly realized that most of my ideas of what God expected of me were not His ideas but rather mine that I had made or picked up through my years growing up in my church. And this was just my freshman year. By the end of that year I had been asked to become the Student Assistant Chaplain to Dr. Fowler, had become a very active member of Baptist Campus Ministries, and had become a Christian Studies minor. My next three years would be huge in my development of who I am now.

During my next three years of college, I grew as a Christian. I discovered that God wanted me to care for the poor and for the downtrodden, not tell them to get a job. I also discovered that my one time a year of "doing good" was not what was wanted. God wanted me to do that all the time and not just because I would look good doing so. This was still a downfall for me. I was still self righteous and considered myself above others. I would still try to make others come to my point of view and force them to see that I was correct and they were wrong, when in reality, what mattered was that we were servants of God and the little differences that we had were, in the long run, nothing.

College was also the place where I began an intellectual breaking of shackles in my faith. For most of my life I took what had been taught at church as gospel and that what was taught was what all Christians believed or should believe. In college, along with the JEPD theory, I learned that church history was not nice and tidy, that theology was anything but uniform and that what I had imagined as coming straight from God through the ages, especially in music, was actually a building upon foundations that had been laid centuries before. This was the time when I learned the Apostle's Creed, when I discovered that Protestants celebrate Lent and Advent, and when it was gently pointed out that Christian Music, aside from Southern Gospel, does not have to come from a hymnal. I also discovered that holiness does not depend upon the list I have made of what is holy.

My journey took a huge leap forward when I went to seminary right after college. I was suddenly thrown into an environment that challenged my beliefs more than I had ever experienced. I discovered that what my church taught regarding eschatology (a new word for me) was known as dispensationalism (another new word for me). I learned this in one of my classes where a professor took it step by step and carefully examined the teachings. I was then convinced that I was no longer a dispensationalist as what the professor said regarding the shortcomings of the beliefs made absolutely perfect sense and was more in line with historic Christianity. I would sit in impromptu discussions in the hallway kitchen or another schoolmate's room and wrestle with the lessons I was learning and with how I had been taught. Most importantly, I began to read the Bible more thoroughly and examine closely where I was and where I had been. It struck me that I had not heard many sermons from the Minor Prophets because they did not teach about Jesus or point to his coming except in a few passages. Rather they taught compassion, justice and doing what God required. This was something that was not really taught at my church. I was discovering that God wanted me and not what I could do for him. I was discovering, in short, that path of being a disciple.

By the time I attended seminary, which I entered in 1995, I had left the church in which I had been raised. Not because of the people nor because they did not teach salvation by grace. I left because they taught that it was their version of grace. That one could only be holy if he followed a certain set of rules. That if one believed evolution was true, that if one believed that the Bible might not be quite as straightforward as was taught, that if a person had doubts, that if a person did not feel an invitation was quite honest in leading to faith in Christ, then that person was suspect in his salvation. I left because I had found a faith that had me cling to God and His grace and holiness only. Did I still struggle? Of course, I did. To this day I struggle with what God wants and what He requires of me. But I know I am His and I am that by His grace.

I am now a member of the United Methodist Church. I still have days and moments where I feel intense guilt because I believe that God is not approving of what I am doing. It is then that I realize I sometimes still have a list of how to be holy that I follow. When this occurs, I remember that it is God's grace I must lean upon and His mercy. My journey from fear to faith has been a rocky one as most are. But I never lost sight of who was the ultimate guide.

My faith today is stronger because of what I went through with my struggle with fear. My wish/mission today is to bring others to a greater understanding of grace that they may not have to move from fear to faith as I have done.

2

CONFRONTING OUR FEARS

MIKE BEIDLER[1]

CONFRONTING OUR FEARS, PART 1: INTRODUCTION

Peace I leave with you; my peace I give to you. Not as the world gives do I give to you. Let not your hearts be troubled, neither let them be afraid. (John 14:27, English Standard Version [ESV])

In 2007, after a turbulent two-year process, I came to embrace evolutionary creationism as the best scientific and theological paradigm through which to view the natural world and God's strategy to redeem humanity from the power of sin. As a layman who possessed neither a degree in the natural sciences nor a degree in

1 Mike Beidler is a commander in the U.S. Navy. He holds an MS in Global Leadership from the University of San Diego, a BA in Political Science from the University of Michigan, and an AA in Persian-Farsi from the U.S. Army's Defense Language Institute. Mike is a member of the American Scientific Affiliation (ASA) and the National Center for Science Education (NCSE). He currently resides in the Washington, D.C., metro area where he works as a Middle East politico-military adviser, runs the popular blog "Rethinking the αlpha and Ωmega," and helps administer the Facebook group Celebrating Creation by Natural Selection.

This essay is adapted from a 5-part series originally published by The BioLogos Foundation during the period November 12-30, 2012. ("Confronting Our Fears," The BioLogos Foundation, accessed January 21, 2013, http://biologos.org/blog/series/confronting-our-fears.)

theology, moving from my long-held young-earth creationist position was not an easy journey. My personal library was already full
of literature arguing for a young-earth creationist position, and I
was intimately familiar with all of the scientific and theological
arguments against theistic evolution. Furthermore, my journey was
relatively private and I knew few others who were traveling a similar path—others who could be fellow sojourners with me through
the various spiritual and intellectual battles that lay ahead. But it
was actually several personal fears that were the greatest enemies
on my path toward the goal of integrating my long-held faith in
Christ with a new understanding of physical world around me. In
a step of faith, I dedicated myself to a robust self-study regimen in
order to help wade through the diverse scientific and theological
issues at hand.

In the end, my Christian faith not only remained intact, my
journey resulted in a richer faith in the divine Logos-made-flesh
(John 1:14); a profound love for the universe created for, by, and
through the pre-existent Christ (Col 1:16; John 1:3); and an in-
creased awe in a God who could accomplish so much "from so
simple a beginning."[2] Over the last five years since I declared publicly my acceptance of the scientific evidence for evolution and
humanity's common ancestry with the rest of Earth's flora and fau-
na,[3] my family and I have been through two work-related moves,
and have belonged to two conservative Christian congregations;
both communities professed and lived out their faith in Jesus
of Nazareth to an admirable degree, and both remain decidedly
young-earth creationist in their theology. In both cases, I chose
not to hide my evolutionary creationist views, but rather discuss
them openly when people solicited my views. In return, I have been

---

2   Charles Darwin, *On the Origin of Species* [1859] in Edward O. Wil-
son, ed., *From So Simple a Beginning: The Four Great Books of Charles
Darwin* (New York: W. W. Norton & Company, 2006), 760.
3   I launched my blog "The Creation of an Evolutionist" in December
2007 and have since renamed it "Rethinking the αlpha and Ωmega"
(http://www.rethinkingao.com).

blessed by a noticeable extension of grace from family, friends, and fellow churchgoers—testimony to the fact that we can live and worship together in unity, even when we disagree over this issue.

Of course, being fully aware of how foreign a theistic evolutionary paradigm is to many an evangelical Christian audience, I've learned to have interactions about my views privately and with the utmost respect for the personal beliefs of my conversation partners—those beliefs are the ones I once held, after all. Furthermore, I've developed a heightened sensitivity to the issue of spiritual maturity, that is, how well-grounded one's faith is in the person of Jesus Christ. As a result, I have had the pleasure of discussing my journey in an atmosphere of genuine mutual admiration with more than a few people in my worship community. Through these various dialogues, I have identified four fears about considering evolutionary creationism that, in most cases, mirrored those I experienced in my own journey. These fears are not petty, nor are they inconsequential. They are real and can have long-lasting effects if not dealt with in love, patience, honesty, and understanding. I'd like to describe and explore those fears and how they might be overcome through Christ, and always with an eye on deeper faith in Him.

Although this essay is written primarily for those who are honestly seeking an integration of scientific truth with their faith in Christ, yet are struggling mightily in the process, it can also serve as an aid to evolutionary creationists who seek to share how one's Christian faith can remain intact, authentic, and vibrant, even during such a paradigm-shifting pilgrimage. It is my prayer that these reflections will assist the reader in identifying such personal fears, spur the genuine seeker to work through the sources of his or her anxieties, and direct him or her toward scholarly, pastoral resources (most always located in the footnotes of this essay) that can assist the acceptance of evolution as God's chosen method of creating. All of this is possible without sacrificing such core tenets of evangelical faith as belief in the role of Jesus in actual history (cf. Luke 1:1-4), the necessity of the Holy Spirit to transcend our fallen natures (Rom 14:17), and the experience of spiritual rebirth as adopted children of God (John 1:12-13; 3:3).

The heart of all anxiety is fear of loss.

CONFRONTING OUR FEARS, PART 2:
LOSING BIBLICAL AUTHORITY

All Scripture is breathed out by God and profitable for teaching, for reproof, for correction, and for training in righteousness, that the man of God may be complete, equipped for every good work. (2 Tim 3:16-17, ESV)

Throughout my various conversations with fellow believers, the most-mentioned anxiety over accepting an evolutionary creationist paradigm is the fear of losing the Bible as one's spiritual anchor and source of authority—the texts that give the global Christian community its doctrinal and philosophical distinctiveness. Growing up in the Baptist tradition and later becoming a member of the Southern Baptist Convention, the inerrancy of "God-breathed"[4] Scripture and its identification as the fount of all truth was paramount in defining my life as a Christian believer. Of course, while some would debate the veracity of such a doctrine as it pertains to this discussion, I believe that neither inerrancy nor authority is at issue when it comes to Genesis' opening chapter. The real issue is *hermeneutics*—how we read the authoritative texts.

An interpretative rule used commonly in evangelical Christian churches today states, "If the literal sense makes good sense, seek no other sense lest you come up with nonsense." This method, however, lends itself unnecessarily to the fear of losing biblical authority. This tendency toward fear is especially acute when the individual doing the interpreting does not have at his or her fingertips the full scope of knowledge required to allow the biblical text to speak for itself—or rather, to allow God to speak through ancient genres with which the interpreter isn't naturally familiar.

---

4   The literal meaning of the Greek word θεόπνευστος (*theopneustos*).

I readily admit that the "literal sense" of Genesis 1—as dictated by our own culture that focuses on material origins and unwittingly holds Genesis 1 hostage to the scientific method—*does in fact rule out* cosmological and biological evolution as God's creative methods. But perhaps a better question would be whether a "literary sense" of Genesis 1 would *allow* for evolution. To read evolution into Scripture (eisegesis) or out of Scripture (exegesis) would be dishonest, especially considering that the author (or final redactor) of Genesis was not privy to modern scientific discoveries. I would also argue that a "literal" reading of Genesis 1, framed by our own modern paradigm, is *unfaithful* to the original intent of the author, and that we should take special care to read Genesis 1 "literarily" through the eyes of the ancient Hebrews, understanding what was (and wasn't) important to them. Dr. Conrad Hyers writes:

> This is the interpretive issue, and it cannot be settled by dogmatic assertions, threats about creeping secularism, or attempts to associate views with skepticism . . . . Nor can the issue be settled by marshaling scientific evidence for or against either evolution or six-day creation, since it would first need to be demonstrated that the Genesis accounts <u>intended</u> to offer scientific and historical statements. Otherwise the whole discussion is based on the wrong premises. As such it is scientific creationism itself which compromises the religious meaning of Genesis and is an accommodation to scientific language and method.[5]

Since Genesis was written in the Hebrew language and most of us can't read Hebrew, we take for granted the necessity of translating from an ancient language into another in which we are fluent. Yet, we often forget that, because we are separated by at least 2,500

---

5   Conrad Hyers, *The Meaning of Creation: Genesis and Modern Science* (Atlanta: John Knox Press, 1984), 26; emphasis in the original.

years from the culture that produced Genesis, we also need the culture "translated" for us as well.[6]

Returning to the text

As I mentioned above, adopting an overly literal hermeneutic strongly lends itself to ruling out both old-earth creationism and theistic evolution, but as a firm believer that "all truth is God's truth," I felt that I was missing something. Because I believed (and still do) that the six days of creation were six, successive, 24-hour periods ("there was evening and there was morning—the nth day"), I struggled mightily to understand Genesis 1 in light of what I had been learning about the vast age of the cosmos as determined by the best scientific minds, both secular and Christian.[7] If the age of the cosmos truly was as old as the scientific establishment has led us to believe, I thought that digging deeper into the culture of the ancient Near East could help me reconcile the two opposing forces of scientific observation and biblical testimony.

It was at this time that I discovered the works of John Walton, Professor of Old Testament at Wheaton College. His commentary on Genesis[8] and his book on the conceptual world of the Hebrew

---

6   John H. Walton, interview. *From the Dust: Conversations in Creation.* Blu-ray Disc. Directed by Ryan Petty. Mountain View, CA: Highway Media and The BioLogos Foundation, 2012.

7   For a secular treatment, see G. Brent Dalrymple, *The Age of the Earth* (Stanford: Stanford University Press, 1994); for evangelical Christian treatments, see Davis A. Young and Ralph F. Stearley, *The Bible, Rocks and Time: Geological Evidence for the Age of the Earth* (Grand Rapids: IVP Academic, 2008); Howard J. Van Till, *The Fourth Day: What the Bible and the Heavens Are Telling Us about the Creation* (Grand Rapids: William B. Eerdmans Publishing Company, 1986); Howard J. Van Till, ed., *Portraits of Creation: Biblical and Scientific Perspectives on the World's Formation* (Grand Rapids: William B. Eerdmans Publishing Company, 1990).

8   John H. Walton, *The NIV Application Commentary: Genesis* (Grand Rapids: Zondervan, 2001).

Scriptures[9] propelled me toward a realization that the focus of Genesis 1 was much less on the material origin of the cosmos and much more on the cosmos' purpose as a functional and purposeful dwelling place for God—a cosmic temple, if you will. Furthermore, his reading actually accentuated mankind's role as representative "image-bearers" of God, as wielders of his authority on Earth. I learned that the symbolism and literary structure of Genesis 1, including the 7-day structure of the creation week, had its roots in an ancient Near Eastern (ANE) cognitive environment that held the concepts of function and purpose to be more important than (but not entirely exclusive of) material origins, the latter of which currently guides our modern, scientific way of thinking. It even reconciled the seemingly contradictory accounts of a weeklong series of creative acts and a 13.8-billion-year-old universe.[10]

With these interpretive tools in hand, I was able to successfully assuage my fear of losing biblical authority insofar as Genesis 1 was concerned, and my openness to evolutionary theory came quite naturally. If the preponderance of scientific evidence adequately explained the existence of all biological organisms, past and present, by evolutionary means, I could accept mainstream evolutionary theory[11] while maintaining the theological authority of the Bible's

---

9 John H. Walton, *Ancient Near Eastern Thought and Old Testament: Introducing the Conceptual World of the Hebrew Bible* (Grand Rapids: Baker Academic, 2006). See also John H. Walton, *The Lost World of Genesis One: Ancient Cosmology and the Origins Debate* (Downers Grove, IL: IVP Academic, 2009); John H. Walton, *Genesis 1 as Ancient Cosmology* (Winona Lake, IN: Eisenbrauns, 2011); Gordon J. Wenham, *Word Biblical Commentary: Genesis 1-15* (Nashville: Thomas Nelson, 1987); Gordon J. Glover, *Beyond the Firmament: Understanding Science and the Theology of Creation* (Chesapeake, VA: Watertree Press, LLC, 2007).

10 A more refined estimate is 13.77 billion years, with an uncertainty of only 0.4%. See "WMAP – Age of the Universe," National Aeronautics and Space Administration (NASA), accessed January 21, 2013, http://map.gsfc.nasa.gov/universe/uni_age.html.

11 See Daniel J. Fairbanks, *Relics of Eden: The Powerful Evidence of Evolution in Human DNA* (Amherst, NY: Prometheus Books, 2007) and

opening chapter. As long as I took pains to bridge the vast cultural gap when attempting to determine the theological message of the text—which God accommodated for the Hebrew culture and chose to express in a culturally bound literary form—I wouldn't need to fear abandoning the Bible as a source of theological truth and spiritual authority. As long as I aimed to let the Bible to speak for itself, using the best biblical scholarship available to determine who wrote the various books of the Bible, to whom they were written, and when they were written, I could have confidence that the end result would be a more faithful pronouncement of what the Bible is actually telling us, millennia later, through ancient voices.

Of course, things are never that easy when it comes to biblical authority. The functional ontology and temple imagery of Genesis 1, as well as its parallels with other ANE creation myths and temple dedication texts, carry over into the next two chapters of Genesis, which feature the creation of Adam and Eve and the entrance of sin and death into the world of mankind. What was I to do with the historicity of Adam and Eve?

If the Hebrew Scriptures stood alone as a source of spiritual authority in my life as a Christian, it wouldn't be much of an issue. I could accept a mythological Adam and Eve within the framework of an etiological account[12] of human origins, but there is this second corpus of literature held sacred by Christians commonly known as the New Testament. As a Christian, I now had an issue with Paul and his clear treatment of Adam as a real person rooted in human history. If that wasn't enough, I was also confronted by the salvific role of Jesus himself. How could an historical, literal Jesus solve the very real problem of sin that resulted from the rebellious act of a mythical, literary Adam?

Keith B. Miller, ed., *Perspectives on an Evolving Creation* (Grand Rapids: William B. Eerdmans Publishing Company, 2003).
12 "Etiology," Wikipedia, accessed October 08, 2012, http://en.wikipedia.org/wiki/Etiology.

CONFRONTING OUR FEARS, PART 3: LOSING OUR SAVIOR

*For if, because of one man's trespass, death reigned through
that one man, much more will those who receive the abundance of
grace and the free gift of righteousness reign in life through the one
man Jesus Christ. Therefore, as one trespass led to condemnation
for all men, so one act of righteousness leads to justification and
life for all men. For as by the one man's disobedience the many
were made sinners, so by the one man's obedience the many will
be made righteous.* (Rom 5:17-19, ESV)

As Christians, we have to take seriously Paul's clear treatment
of Adam as a real person rooted in human history. Furthermore,
Paul seems to have thought that an historical Adam was important
not for its own sake, but for the logic of salvation through Christ
Jesus. How could an historical, literal Jesus solve the very real problem of sin that resulted from the rebellious act of a mythical, literary
Adam? While that question makes a lot of sense on the surface, are
these two figures as closely linked as I, and many others, think they
are? Before I address whether the connection between Adam and
Jesus is iron-clad or tenuous, though, I need to briefly address a
different common objection heard by evolutionary creationists: If
we accept that the cosmology and anthropology of Genesis 1-3 isn't
accurate from a modern scientific perspective, then we can't trust
the remainder of Scripture. Are we truly on a slippery slope toward
rejecting everything else in Scripture, to include the necessity of
Jesus' role as humanity's redeemer? I don't believe so, and here's why.

As an evolutionary creationist and a Christian, I hold the Bible
to be sacred literature, and I identify fully with the faith community that the Hebrew and Christian Scriptures not only shaped,
but which also shaped the content of Scripture. As a truth-seeker,
I desire to understand what the text is truly saying as much as any
other member of our shared faith. I want to read the Bible for all it
is worth, and that requires taking the time to determine the author's
original intent for *every* passage of Scripture, including various
passages within the same book that were written utilizing different

genres. In doing so, we discover that the literary manner in which the life of Jesus is presented in the four Gospels is nothing like the etiological myths encountered in Genesis 1-11; we can safely treat the Gospels as a reliable source for knowing how the early Church viewed the historical person of Jesus of Nazareth, whose very existence is also documented in extra-biblical literature.

Skeptics of evolutionary creationism may accept that the faith-filled life of a theistic evolutionist is evidence that the Bible still wields moral authority in his or her life, and even that he or she affirms the historicity of the God-man Jesus. But there is often still considerable concern over how evolutionary creationists can affirm the historical assertion that Jesus' death upon the Roman cross was *necessary* if Adam truly never lived and breathed. If Adam never lived (so the argument goes), sin is illusory, atonement for mankind's sin unnecessary, and Jesus' death all the more tragic. Because the person of Jesus *and* His sacrifice is so central to the Christian faith, *this is a valid fear*. However, I believe this fear can be dissected carefully and ultimately overcome once one acknowledges that, even without an original source and propagator of sin (i.e., Adam), the sinfulness of mankind (1) remains universally observable and repeatable, (2) can be explained as a result of our status as a created species with free will and a genetic predisposition to sin inherited from our ancestors, and (3) is still recognized as an inherent moral weakness that needs correction and redemption (if a divine lawgiver is presumed). All this, even if Adam and Eve were not historical persons co-complicit in an historical "fall." In fact, one could argue that evolutionary biology provides an even more powerful paradigm for explaining the source of mankind's sinful nature in our day than the biblical text does.

Many evolutionary creationists are convinced that our inherited evolutionary baggage—borne of an instinctual (and once necessary) need to preserve one's self by means of selfish acts—still requires divine intervention in order to allow us to altruistically transcend what Paul calls the "flesh" (Rom 7:18; 8:5-9). We still need the work of the Holy Spirit to lead us on a sanctifying path to make us more than merely human and increasingly like the Logos of whom John the Baptist testified (John 1:6-8).[13]

An historical Adam

One can certainly argue that Paul treated Adam as an historical person. Yes, I believe Paul certainly did; but this is to be expected and readily admitted.[14] To believe that God created Adam approximately 4,000 years before Paul's day was an integral part of the Jews' religious heritage. Paul's belief that Adam actually existed is a natural extension of his rigid upbringing in the Pharisaical tradition. Nevertheless, Paul was not attempting to make an anthropological point and arguing for the necessity of a literal Adam; he was making a soteriological one and defending the necessity for a literal Savior. Even if Paul knew better by exclusive revelation from the Holy Spirit, Paul's appropriation of Adam's original act of rebellion is, of course, perfectly acceptable since, regardless of sin's "material" origin, the solution to mankind's sin problem remains Jesus' sacrificial act—an act of love that requires a particular *context* for it to "make sense" to those to whom Paul preached.

Anticipating the claim that Paul, an inspired apostle, would not have used the rebellious act of a mythical person to justify the loving act of an historical one, I can only appeal to the argument that theological truths need not be couched in the dry, straightforward manner of modern journalism. God can (and did!) inspire the authors of Scripture to express His truths through a variety of methods: myth, legend, epic, poetry, wisdom literature, historical narrative, gospel, pastoral letters, and apocalyptic literature. Jesus' parables even featured actors who never existed and

---

13 See Daryl P. Domning and Monika K. Hellwig, *Original Selfishness: Original Sin and Evil in the Light of Evolution* (Burlington, VT: Ashgate Publishing Company, 2006).

14 For other possible ways to understand Paul's understanding of Adam, see Peter Enns, *The Evolution of Adam: What the Bible Says and Doesn't Say about Human Origins* (Grand Rapids: Brazos Press, 2012).

utilized historical fiction to press his points. Sometimes truth is best communicated through means that accommodate our current paradigms (as inaccurate as they may be) and meet us where we are. All genres that illuminate truth are the "best kinds," and God uses story as well as history to illuminate His truth.

Next, we'll continue our exploration of fears that I and other evangelicals have about considering evolutionary creation by looking at the fear of losing face.

Confronting Our Fears, Part 4: Losing Face

Here is an extended (and possibly familiar) quote from Augustine about what's at stake when we ask, "What if I'm wrong?"

> Usually, even a non-Christian knows something about the earth, the heavens, and the other elements of this world, about the motion and orbit of the stars and even their size and relative positions, about the predictable eclipses of the sun and moon, the cycles of the years and the seasons, about the kinds of animals, shrubs, stones, and so forth, and this knowledge he holds to as being certain from reason and experience.
>
> Now, it is a disgraceful and dangerous thing for an infidel to hear a Christian, presumably giving the meaning of Holy Scripture, talking nonsense on these topics; and we should take all means to prevent such an embarrassing situation, in which people show up vast ignorance in a Christian and laugh it to scorn. The shame is not so much that an ignorant individual is derided, but that people outside the household of faith think our sacred writers held such opinions, and, to the great loss of those for whose salvation we toil, the writers of our Scripture are criticized and rejected as unlearned men.
>
> If they find a Christian mistaken in a field which they themselves know well and hear him maintaining his foolish opinions about our books, how are they going to believe those books in matters concerning the resurrection of the dead, the hope of eternal life, and the kingdom of heaven, when they think their pages are full of falsehoods and on facts which they themselves have learnt from experience and the light of reason?

Reckless and incompetent expounders of Holy Scripture bring untold trouble and sorrow on their wiser brethren when they are caught in one of their mischievous false opinions and are taken to task by those who are not bound by the authority of our sacred books. For then, to defend their utterly foolish and obviously untrue statements, they will try to call upon Holy Scripture for proof and even recite from memory many passages which they think support their position, although they understand neither what they say nor the things about which they make assertion.[15]

– St. Augustine of Hippo (AD 354-430)

For a good portion of my life, I had an extremely difficult time admitting that I was wrong. To do so was an admission of intellectual failure, faulty logic, or simple *ignorance*—not knowing everything about everything.[16] Being wrong is a hard pill to swallow sometimes, because in many cases it equates to losing face. As it pertains to the creation-evolution debate, I believe that we evangelical Christians tend to express that fear by "holding the line" against certain areas of scientific study, rather than being willing to admit that we might be wrong. In most cases, we have no problem accepting the authority of the world's best physicists, chemists, meteorologists, engineers, and physicians. Our problem tends to be with scientific authorities in only certain areas of study, such as biology, anthropology, paleontology, geology, and astronomy. Why? It's because the Bible is the divinely inspired word of God and these areas conflict with the plain reading of Scripture, right?

When we evangelicals come to the table of scientific discussion, we tend to pick and choose those "foods" which appeal to us, while wrinkling our noses at what our theological tastes find disagreeable. As long as the menu includes a wide assortment of

15 St. Augustine of Hippo, *The Literal Meaning of Genesis* (*De Genesi ad litteram*), Trans. J. H. Taylor, in *Ancient Christian Writers* (Long Prairie, MN: Newman Press, 1982), vol. 41.
16 "Ignorant," Oxford Dictionaries, accessed October 08, 2012, http://oxforddictionaries.com/definition/english/ignorant.

things we already like, and we share the table with people with similar tastes, we can get along just fine with this strategy. But is this wise in, say, a survival situation? Food is food, and if we're hungry enough and don't have a life-threatening allergic reaction to something specific, I would venture to guess that we'd dig right in without a second thought. In regard to the creation-evolution debate, I am convinced that the evangelical church will find itself in dire straights if we intentionally starve ourselves intellectually, especially with a healthy banquet in full sight and within reach. I also think having a too-restricted "diet" limits our ability to sit down with those outside the church and can, as Augustine believed, play a role in actually prohibiting the secular world at large from coming to a saving knowledge of Christ, "to the great loss of those for whose salvation we toil." Several years ago, Bruce Waltke, former Evangelical Theological Society president and former professor of Old Testament at Dallas Theological Seminary, updated Augustine's caution in a brief video production for BioLogos, suggesting that the church risks losing our ability to really interact with the world if we don't trust God's providence in this area.[17] Wheaton College's Professor of Christian Thought, Mark Noll, as the very first sentence of his book *The Scandal of the Evangelical Mind* writes, "The scandal of the evangelical mind is that there is not much of an evangelical mind."[18] If not for the fact that I've never met Professor Noll, I'd believe he was talking about me a decade ago.

What drives us evangelical Christians to "hold the line" against acknowledging truths in these certain categories of scientific knowledge? After undergoing several theological shifts myself over the last decade, and seeing others do the same, I believe I've been able to "reverse engineer" what happened in my own life: It was a subtle slide from a confident faith into a comfortable, unwitting arro-

---

17 "Why Must the Church Come to Accept Evolution?" The BioLogos Foundation, accessed November 12, 2102, http://biologos.org/blog/why-must-the-church-come-to-accept-evolution.
18 Mark A. Noll, *The Scandal of the Evangelical Mind* (Grand Rapids: William B. Eerdmans Publishing Company, 1994), 3.

gance. When we believe that we are in an intimate spiritual union with the Creator of the universe, it's quite easy to forget (if we ever understood this in the first place) that God can couch theological truth in a variety of literary genres and, yes, even in the context of ancient, scientifically inaccurate cosmologies.[19] Caught up in the awesome truth of spiritual union, what makes perfect sense to us at any particular point in our spiritual walk can be easily confused with "*the* truth." We also gravitate toward churches that conform to our particular belief systems. We prefer pastors who preach to the choir. We buy books that support our particular theological system. To attend another church, listen to a theologically edgy pastor, or read a book from a completely opposite viewpoint from what we're accustomed to would be to invite a considerable measure of tension into an otherwise comfortable intellectual and spiritual environment.

How many of us actually have or take the time to study evolutionary biology, theology, the history of biblical interpretation, ANE literature, or modern translations of Babylonian creation myths? I would venture to guess that very few of us have the same opportunities that professional scientists and theologians take for granted in their academic careers. To overcome the fear of losing intellectual face, I recommend exposing oneself to different ways of thinking about these topics, including perspectives that you might deem "outside the box." Reading multi-view comparisons and critiques, such as those found in Zondervan's wonderful Counterpoints series,[20] is particularly helpful in this regard. Familiarity with and exposure to these views helps temper that initial fear or

---

19 See Denis Lamoureux, *Evolutionary Creation: A Christian Approach to Evolution* (Eugene, OR: Wipf and Stock Publishers, 2008); Brian Godawa, "Mesopotamian Cosmic Geography in the Bible," The BioLogos Foundation, accessed October 04, 2012, http://biologos.org/uploads/projects/godawa_scholarly_paper_2.pdf.

20 See Zondervan.com, search results for books in the Counterpoints series, accessed October 04, 2012, http://zondervan.com/products?-search_text=views.

shock when we come across those few brothers and sisters in Christ who opt to take another approach to any one topic. (One youth pastor friend of mine, when discovering my views on a particular topic, approached me and excitedly exclaimed that meeting me was like meeting a dragon: "You hear stories about them, but you never see one!")

A word of warning: Before I adopted evolutionary creationism, my neatly packed theology was virtually stress-free. Ignorance was truly bliss. Then came the paradigm shift, and all sorts of previously suppressed tension, questions, and doubts rose to the surface. Another word of warning: If you're *not* confronted with tension, questions, and doubts in your day-to-day spiritual walk, something's wrong. Wrestling with theological issues is not an activity to be avoided; it is a discipline to be vigorously pursued! If you are comfortable enough in your relationship with the risen Savior, you should not fear admitting your ignorance on various topics and entering into a period of temporary uncertainty.[21] This fear can be remedied by taking advantage of a fully informed palette of theological options provided by genuine Jesus followers, including those that embrace biblical criticism. If one's faith is truly rooted in the One by, for, and through Whom all things were made, all the theories put forth by the higher biblical critics and esoteric scientists should be no cause for fear—but all should be cause for loving dialogue.

---

21 See Daniel Taylor, *The Myth of Certainty: The Reflective Christian & the Risk of Commitment* (Downer's Grove, IL: InterVarsity Press, 1992) and the chapter "Epistemology and Hermeneutics" in Kenton L. Sparks, *God's Word in Human Words: An Evangelical Appropriation of Critical Biblical Scholarship* (Grand Rapids: Baker Academic, 2008), 25-55.

CONFRONTING OUR FEARS, PART 5: LOSING PEACE

Who shall separate us from the love of Christ? Shall tribulation, or distress, or persecution, or famine, or nakedness, or danger, or sword? (Rom 8:35, ESV)

Eight times in 21 years, my work has required that I pull up stakes and move. And with every new work-related move has come the loss of a loving church family and the dreaded journey of finding a new church home. For someone like me, that's not an easy task. Though I've been asked on a number of occasions why I don't seek out a church that agrees with what I believe theologically in regard to creation and evolution, the fact is that conservative, evangelical churches are a "known quantity" in each location in which we've lived—dependable places to find Christian community, and ones with which I've never desired to part. Also, if I took only and all of my theology into account, I'd end up worshiping in a church comprised of just me: a cult of one! But worshiping the Trinitarian God is to be done in community, and theology is something to be lived out in that community—not simply studied. Thus, my family and I have chosen not to isolate ourselves with others who agree with us on every point of Christian culture; we go where the Holy Spirit leads, and it appears that God's found fit to put us right in the middle of congregations that are solidly young-earth creationist—right in the middle of all sorts of potential anxiety.

Depending on your particular situation, loss of peace can come in a variety of forms. It can be well-intentioned but overbearing counseling from concerned pastors and elders who fear the entrance of heresy into the church. It can be shunning by other families in your homeschooling circle. It can be the internal heartache caused by shocked family members and the resultant emotional discord that follows when your theological views no longer align with those of your spouse. It can be the threat of joblessness if your employer finds out that its premiere Old Testament scholar has shifted his views away from the institution's Doctrinal Statement of Faith. It can be the threat of losing your entire apologetics ministry because a vast majority of your supporters will no longer support you if you revealed your paradigm shift. It can be the potential financial loss resulting from a repudiation of your previous scholarly work. One does not easily step out of the comfort zone of seemingly-settled doctrine into a world in which one's beliefs, if made public, can cause all sorts of worry or anger from family members, pastors, friends, co-workers, and supporters.

As I mentioned in the introduction, church members, pastors, elders, and deacons have blessed me by *not* causing me to endure any significant persecution. So what's the secret? I'm not entirely sure. While I'm careful not to reveal my entire hand at the first available opportunity, I've never hidden or denied my views, either. In fact, when my wife and I last attempted to pursue official church membership, the board of elders denied our membership request as a result of my evolutionary creationist views. Nonetheless, we were warmly welcomed into the life of the congregation: My wife was given a children's Sunday school teaching position, and I joined the worship team as a vocalist. More amazing to me was that I was explicitly instructed not to refrain from discussing my views if the occasion should arise—even within the context of adult Bible studies. Was the invitation to continued fellowship (if not membership) in our church the fruit of candidly confessing my views before the church's elder board? Was it because I had exemplified my devotion to Jesus Christ in the months previous? Or was it demonstrating a thorough knowledge of Scripture that invited a congenial spirit from those whom I believed would firmly oppose me? Perhaps it was a combination of all of the above. This same approach of demonstrating respect and love before, during, and after engaging in risky dialogue has also proved successful with interactions in our current congregation, and we find ourselves once again fully involved in various church activities and ministries despite not being voting members of the church body. In every case, my agenda is nothing more than to be a productive member of the Body of Christ.

Although my "layman's advice" doesn't necessarily translate to a sure-fire method of maintaining a teaching position at a Christian academic institution, keeping an apologetics-based ministry afloat, or maintaining your book sales, I do know that attitudes and actions that reflect a devotion to Jesus win over hearts (if not minds), and are vastly superior to argumentative behavior and being a constant source of dissension. Granted, not all churches will be as accommodating as mine, but I offer my anecdotes as a small measure of hope for those readers who have encountered or will likely encounter persecution from family, friends, and fellow brothers and sisters in Christ. Whatever your situation is, treat those who persecute you with love, patience, and understanding, and reassure them of your steadfast devotion to Jesus Christ. If your Christ-like love isn't returned after a concerted effort on your part to forestall a spiritually bloody confrontation, shake the dust off your feet and move on to a congregation that will accept you (cf. Matt 10:14). You owe it to yourself and those who rely upon you for spiritual leadership and protection.

Finally, I would also counsel those who stop pursuing the truth for fear of losing peace in their lives to not succumb to that fear. Rest on Jesus' promise that the truth will set you free (John 8:32). Seek the help of the Lord (Heb 13:6) and seek the help of those who are on or have successfully made the same journey. We are out there, we love you, and we will help you (Gal 6:2).

> *Have no fear of them, nor be troubled, but in your hearts honor Christ the Lord as holy, always being prepared to make a defense to anyone who asks you for a reason for the hope that is in you; yet do it with gentleness and respect, having a good conscience, so that, when you are slandered, those who revile your good behavior in Christ may be put to shame.* (1 Pet 3:14b-16, ESV)

3

THE JOY OF CONFESSION

REV. SHANNON MURRAY

"Really?!" she blurted, surprised that the internal thought had escaped her lips. Everyone else just sat there, stared for a moment, realized that was rude and diverted their eyes. From the other side of the mammoth round table, following the uncomfortable silence came, "Never would've guessed it," accompanied by a few grunts of agreement and then, like it never happened, the Bible study conversation moved on to apparently less shocking topics, like God's use of Balaam's donkey. How could I have fooled them so thoroughly? I suspect this was the real question on their minds; how could someone in the inner circle, a leader and preacher, a candidate for ordination have ever not been a part of a church, much less questioned whether or not they believed in God at all?

This was my first naïve leap into radical, expectant, theological praxis. In this year-long Bible study, we'd talked a great deal about how God had a preference for using people who were, well, a hot mess and how Jesus came for the sinners, spending time with prostitutes and tax collectors, etc., but when a real life, flesh and blood former-heathen showed up in their midst, the faithful revealed that they thought nowadays God still used sinners, you know, the ones in the churches, but those outside the walls were surely beyond help. I don't know that they ever looked at me the same after that but neither did the fourteen people who came forward to be baptized the first time I ever gave an altar call, most of whom had heard the same story; the one where I dispel the myth that all pastors spring forth from the womb wearing a robe and utter the Nicene

Creed as their first words. The same truth provoked (and continues to provoke) two very different reactions; what rattled some would reassure others. One big difference is that the latter group (and those like them) asked questions, often over meals. "How did it happen? How did you know that Jesus loved you? That he could forgive you?" They wanted to believe it was possible. They needed to believe it was possible and I need to be continually reminded of it too. In proclaiming the freedom Christ had given me to those who longed to be free, I stopped thinking I was a fly in the ointment and realized I was leaven in the loaf. That's when I began to embrace the joy of confessing who I was in order to celebrate fully who I've become and invite others to the party.

In the inner circle, the church-goer bubble, most everyone I'd encountered had been raised in the church. I had met a few people who had not always believed but they all seemed to know the date when they were "saved" and would ask me when it happened for me. I always struggled to answer because it didn't happen all at once for me. This confused me in the beginning, filled me with doubt at one point and then became a point of huge frustration. I recall at one point filling out a form for an organization that asked for the date I was saved; I'm not sure that my answer, "Approximately 33 AD", was what they had in mind but like I said, I was frustrated. For me, it was and is a process. I'm still becoming, growing, stumbling, learning, and honestly, I am a little prickly around folks who feel like they don't need to do any of that because they have arrived (if I recall correctly, I think Jesus had some strong words for folks like that but anyway, on with my story …)

I was blind to it at the time, but looking back, I can see that God was tapping me on the shoulder throughout my life, always present and offering wisdom but letting me choose whether or not to listen; unfortunately the world had to deal me several blows to the head before I would. My earliest recollection of this was at age four. I was born to an eighteen year old mother and an alcoholic father who divorced in my infancy. My mother and I were then living with my great-grandparents whom had raised her. My family was the type that thought the church was nothing but a bunch of judgmental hypocrites and so you could believe in God and love Jesus but you didn't have to go to church. Also, you never brought Jesus up in regular conversation; that was rude. Yet in spite of this, there was a constant presence of Christ in our house in the form of a sepia tone Jesus painting on the living room wall; you know the one that is standard issue décor for every elderly folks Sunday school room you have ever been in? Yeah, that one. He had hung there since before my birth, right over the loveseat, a camouflage Christ in browns and beiges nearly blending in with the faux wood paneling and staring off at the television as if deeply contemplating the wonder of rabbit ear antennas. I first noticed him, really saw him, when I was in preschool and I became mesmerized by this Messiah in my midst; how could I have missed him all these years? When I had asked who was in the painting, my Papa gently said, "Well baby, that's Jesus." I was a bit obsessed with and even a little afraid of this presence and I was a tad uncomfortable under his constant gaze. I became overwhelmed with a need to somehow acknowledge that he was there even though no one ever talked about him, as a painting or otherwise. And so, when no one was around, often late a night, I would go to the doorway of my room, which faced his loveseat altar squarely and quietly, without knowing why, I would kneel with my face pressed into the matted, musty, burnt-orange shag carpet and feel overwhelmed with peace.

Peace was harder to come by in the years that followed. We moved away, my grandparents died, the painting and the farmhouse faded from memory and my childhood was filled with frequent moves, a series of new daddy-figures, my mother's battle with alcohol, the realization that we were poor and the multitude of stuggles that entailed. I kept my grades up and my eyes fixed on getting through and getting out. There was so much pain in those years (the details of which I will spare you) that I just focused on surviving to get to what was next. Then next came, but it wasn't any better. College was even more confusing than home had been; I had known what to do to survive in that system but in college

I completely lost myself. I was trying to be so many things to so many people that I didn't know who I was. If childhood was about scraping my way up and out, college was the free-fall from whatever height I thought I had attained. Raped my freshman year and battling anxiety/depression by graduation, I had become a shell of a person. I was going through the motions, convinced that life was all about doing and having and sure there was never going to be enough to satisfy either goal. My teenage agnostic bent was now bordering on atheism. I was decidedly and willfully numb. So what to do? Repeat my pattern, of course; focus on what is next because surely it's going to get better, right? You could literally insert my previous sentences here: "I kept my grades up and my eyes fixed on getting through and getting out. There was so much pain in those years (the details of which I will spare you) that I just focused on surviving to get to what was next. Then next came, but it wasn't any better."

Partying and working a dead end job was all there was to life after graduation. At this point I no longer even realized I was in free fall; movement is sensed relative to something else but my surroundings had become one continuous blur; I had lost all perspective and context, my very sense of self. I was no longer questioning if God was real, I wasn't sure life was real and if it was, it was of no real importance and had no real purpose. Just a series of events to which I was attached, life was an endless cycle: do, complete, and move on to what is next. So boys and girls, what comes next? Ah yes, first comes love (and college) … then comes marriage … then comes baby in the baby carriage! So goes the playground song and so it was for me. I would keep moving toward what was next but, as the saying goes, wherever you go, there you are and so next was never better and never satisfied the longing inside me for something real.

There was a moment when I was pregnant with our first son that "next" brought about a stirring of sorts. I decided one day that the next thing after a baby is born is a baptism; I had planned to return to the no-church-needed-just-love-God pattern of my family of origin, since we were about to become a family and all, but I also wanted to incorporate my husband's family pattern which included baptizing babies (you could say they are one notch above my family and fall into the used-to-go-to-church-but-now-go-just-for-Christmas-and-Easter category (aka C & E-ers)). But there was an issue, I couldn't ask for the baby to be baptized if I hadn't been baptized myself; the vows wouldn't make sense. So I told my great-aunt, who called the pastor in her small town where my great-grandparents had lived, who agreed to baptize me (and her while he was at it) and even agreed to do it in private (I suspect that all this was in part because he was so thrilled to put two professions of faith down on his charge conference paperwork that year; this sort of thing doesn't happen very often in a town with a population of 127 and two new souls, in terms of population ratios, is a veritable Billy Graham Crusade. I include this little side note because I find it both ironic and sadly funny for those who know the joys of denominational statistics and realize that I am now serving as a mainline denomination pastor; perhaps God does have a sense of humor.) So I was baptized and the vow, well, it kind of started to work on me and make me think and then there was the water; though I cannot really explain it, as it was poured on my head, it did not feel normal; something was different. In hindsight, I see how God began to take this opportunity to get His foot in my door and even though I did not fully realize it, I was marked, set apart, and He was not about to give up on me.

So, what's next? Have the baby. It had been a very rough pregnancy and I had been incredibly ill (again, sparing you the details) so we braced ourselves for complications, and they came. An emergency C-section came first, then the developmental delays by 6 month, the seizures started at 8 months old, then we were told it might be genetic and wind up causing permanent brain damage; oh, and that's also right when we found out we were pregnant again. Suddenly next was not only lacking in satisfaction, it was filled with fear. I did not want what was next anymore. I was terrified, not only because I had one potentially very sick baby and another on the way but because all my hope had always been in what was next and now, for the first time, I knew next was going to be awful. This was the beginning of my "rock bottom". My way, my pattern for survival no longer worked, no longer made any sense. It was not going to get better going forward; going back or staying put were not options either. I had no control and I was suddenly aware that the ground, which had escaped my attention during my free fall, was fast approaching, so close I could count the blades of grass. What do I do? What do I do? What do I do? Like a record skipping in my head, I asked myself this question in a frantic state of panic for weeks, months.

There was nothing I could do but I could not believe that; that would mean I had failed and I never failed. I always moved to what was next but now, the definition of next had changed; someone had changed the rules mid-game and it wasn't fair. I got angry, mostly at myself, then at God, the doctors, anyone within earshot. It was exhausting and it only got worse. Our second son was born incredibly sick with a bacterial infection and coded several times. The weeks in the NICU are a blur and I do not even remember what, if anything I thought of God; I just recall the question, "why?" Why was this happening to our older son? Why this now for our newborn? Why were babies dying in the NICU? Why had any of the terrible things that had happened to me, or anyone else for that matter, ever happened? I moved from anger to despair.

Eventually, we brought our son home but over this milestone and everything else was hanging this fear; what would the future hold for me, for us? Running on fumes a few months later, I took our 20 month old to the children's hospital two hours away to be sedated for an MRI and to be fitted with a multitude of wires he must wear for a 24 hour EEG. When I got there, I was told I could not go in with him. That was it, one of those moments when you feel yourself break. He was screaming and I just stood there, watching the bay doors close. I must have wandered down the hall but I don't remember arriving at the sign that pointed to the chapel. Yet there it was, to my left so I walked into the room. There, on the wall in back, was a painting; a sepia Jesus. I turned away, overwhelmed, angry, scared, exhausted, confused, and I dropped to my knees, sobbing uncontrollably. A woman came in, saying nothing that I can recall, but instead bent down next to me and with her arm around me she simply remained. I have no idea how long we knelt there or who she was but after a time she hugged me and smiled. I nodded, trying to say I would be all right. Then as I stood, I felt a bit of that peace I had experienced, just a bit, just enough to assure me that even though my prayer had had no words, God somehow heard it.

This would perhaps make a better story if I could say, "From that day forward I felt God's presence and I decided to surrender all my fears over, and everything was so much better ...," but I'd be lying. You see I was, like so many, stubborn and stiff-necked. I would take steps forward but only very slowly; oftentimes without realizing they were God-directed until years later; I would call it a "gut feeling" or something dismissive like that. Eventually, over a few years, I became more and more hopeful and grateful as the children's health improved, the seizures stopped and fears of a genetic disorder were put to rest.

The shift that had begun when I was four, that had lay dormant for years, that had stirred in unlikely ways and under painful circumstances slowly but steadily began to increase in its pace and scope. I moved from a rhetorical, angry questioning, "God, what are You doing?!", to a place where the tone changed to pleading and longing, "God, what are You doing?" When the autism diagnosis came for our oldest and then, through incredible therapy and medical interventions he eventually recovered, I thought, "Maybe God is doing." And when, for no apparent reason we felt compelled to move from Massachusetts to the Carolinas and I was faced with knowing practically no one, I finally started asking, "God, what should I do?" It was there that we connected to a church for the first time in our marriage and I began a rapid learning and growing process; it was like a wildfire that had smoldered for a long time had finally caught a good gust of holy wind. I moved into leadership roles and began to sense a call to ministry. My husband's life was transformed before my eyes and we began pursuing the steps necessary for me to answer my call after our third son was born, healthy. There was seminary and my first appointment as a pastor; the many trials that all this entailed where at times seemingly insurmountable but the joys were tremendous as well. I finally went from planning what was next at the cost of the present to finding joy in the day at hand and waiting with excited expectation to see what God had next. Then, when the storms in my life came, which they did and continued to do, I finally started asking, "God, what are we going to do?" At last I realized that I was neither alone, nor a puppet; I was walking with God; the God who caught me inches from the ground when my parachutes failed and had patiently, persistently worked to reveal the truth that had always been there, that He had always been there.

Just like my four-year-old self, I am mesmerized by the Messiah in my midst and I wonder how I could have missed him all those years. I look back over it all today, from this point in my journey where I often feel like an unwelcomed prophet in the inner circle, where I often literally weep for the brokenness of the church, where I struggle to honor my call to be a wife, a mother, and a pastor, where the demands and struggles are endless and the resources and time seem scarce, and I realize that I could not be where I am and hold the hope that I have had I not come from and through so much pain and brokenness. There is such joy in confessing my brokenness to the broken; I know this is how God has worked all those things for good.

I admit I still often feel overwhelmed, unsure, confused, and life has not gotten miraculously easier for us. But now, when I feel myself filling with fear or doubt, I close my eyes and see a sepia Jesus come to life: The browns and beiges turn to crimson stains and his handsome face takes on the reality of one less remarkable, though badly beaten. His eyes close, then open, and he is no longer looking far way but right at me. His wounds heal before my eyes. His hand is upon my shoulder, his peace washes over me, and he knows that in my heart I still long to acknowledge he is there, even in places where people don't talk about him. He is alive and at last, so am I.

4

EXCURSUS – KING JAMES ONLYISM

But those who at this time are going on to perfection proceed very differ-
ently and with quite another temper of spirit; for they progress by means
of humility and are greatly edified, not only thinking naught of their own
affairs, but having very little satisfaction with themselves; they consider all
others as far better, and usually have a holy envy of them, and an eagerness
to serve God as they do.

– JOEL L. WATTS

I have chosen to place this here due to the prevalent use of the
King James Version Bible in fundamentalism.

The year 1611 saw the publication of the Authorized Version,
or in the common vernacular, the King James Version. It was not
the first English bible, and could not truly be separated from those
which had preceded it. After all, it was little more than a revision
called for and brought forth to meet immediate political concerns
and yet, it thrived when other translations faded into the dustbins
of history. It has since become a hallmark to a former time, a way
to combat modern scholarship and in some ways, a preservation
of an ethnocentric view of Scripture. Within the last century or
so, there has arisen a distinct theological belief that it was the only
inspired version of the Bible to be used. This essay will examine
the history of the King James Version along with the rise of the
King James Only movement with special attention to the recent
addition to the movement of the so-called Pure Text (Cambridge)
Edition believers. Further, it will examine the comparisons between
the KJVO movement and the fight against the creation of the English Bible, namely by Wycliffe and Tyndale. We will close with an
examination of future trajectories.

The internet has, without doubt, aided the KJVO movement. Throughout this paper, where books can be cited, they will be; however, most of the discussions from proponents of KJV Only-ism have found a wide reaching pulpit from which to spew their pseudo-scholarly assault on anyone who is, as one KJVO apologist puts it, a "Bible agnostic." To that end, most citations will be from the internet. There are groups, such as the King James Only Debate site, which have devoted some attention to fighting the good fight as it were, but for the most part, scholars and theologians tend to shy away from interacting with the KJVO crowd as they do with most other cults.[1] James White, a Reformed Pastor and Theologian who has authored several works on the subject does regularly engage the KJVO movement, and they in turn often attack him.[2] The KJVO doctrine is not limited to one sect or church. While more often, Independent Fundamentalist Baptists are KJVO, so too are Oneness Holiness sects as well as some United Pentecostal Churches. In many parts of West Virginia and Kentucky, United Methodist Churches continue to be KJV Only.

In King James Only (KJVO) circles, names like Peter Ruckman, Gail Riplinger, and Will Kinney are widely known as purveyors of what a real bible is.[3] Since the publication of *Our Authorized Bible Vindicated* in 1930 by a Seventh-day Adventist the KJVO movement has progressed throughout Christian fundamentalism to solidify a staunch opposition to any new Bible translation and

1   http://kjvonlydebate.com/; Is it fair to describe the KJVO movement as a cult? The basic definition of a cult includes the two tenets of being an unorthodox or spurious sect as well as a group having a singular devotion to some person or some object.

2   See James White, *King James Only Controversy, The: Can You Trust Modern Translations?* (Grand Rapids: Bethany House) 2009

3   The purpose of this paper is not to analyze the people behind the movement, but we must consider the hypocrisy of holding Gail Riplinger up as a leader. The KJVO circle is as a whole restrictive when it comes to women in the ministry as well as anyone divorced. Riplinger, a woman, is on her third marriage. This is only the start of the hypocrisies which surround this movement.

often involves anti-Catholicism and other bigotry. It is rooted in myths of pure texts, hidden bibles, and Satanic attempts to destroy the Word of God. Yet, it strangely mirrors the fight Jerome was presented with in the late fourth century and the same fight which cost the great saint of the English bible, William Tyndale, his life. As with each shift in Christianity, the fear of a loss of power becomes evident. Losing the Septuagint to the Hebrew must have felt like a loss of connection to the Apostles. The battles between Thomas More and William Tyndale, fueled by King Henry VIII, symbolized the great cultural shift in Europe during the time of the Reformation which saw a loosening of hierarchical control by both Church and State. This should frame the discussion on the rise of the KJVO movement, a discussion which sees a rise in equality of women and minorities, the rise in education levels, and a loosening of English ties in North America.

For the sake of this paper, we will forgo a discussion on the literary battles between Augustine and Jerome over basing the Vulgate on the Hebrew instead of the traditional Septuagint. Instead, we will use this time to highlight the journey from the Vulgate to the King James Version of 1611. Beginning nearly one thousand years after the authorization of the revisions to the Old Latin, John Wycliff, an early English reformer, began to have produced, in his name, hand written English translations of the Latin Vulgate which became property of the common people. It would be almost a hundred fifty years later that William Tyndale first produced his New Testament translation from the Greek text prepared by Erasmus. By 1534, the New Testament had been revised by Tyndale and was making inroads into England. His death in 1536 slowed, but did not stop, a full translation into English. In 1535, the Coverdale Bible was issued which made use of Tyndale and Luther's German. This was expanded with Tyndale's translation of some of the Old Testament when John Rogers published his bible in 1537. Several other English translations were issued until the Geneva Bible in

1560 and the Bishop's Bible in 1568.[4] All were still making much use of the Tyndale New Testament and his portions of the Old Testament. After a return to Anglicanism, it was King James IV of Scotland who was also the first of that name to sit upon the English throne, who ordered an authorized version to combat the attacks upon his sovereignty made by the notes in the Geneva Bible. Seven years later, with the Tyndale Version still supplying much of it, the King James Version, or more properly a revision, was born, complete with the Apocrypha.[5] It was not until 1885 with the publication of the Revised Version (followed in 1901 by the American Standard Version) that the King James became severely challenged as the bible for the English speaking peoples.

Like the 1611 version, the Revised Version is also authorized by the English throne, but it never received the same traction. Even with the 1901 release of the American Standard Version, the King James still reigned supreme. In 1930, a book was released which forever established the quintessential myth of the King James Version. Benjamin Wilkinson was a fundamental Seventh-day Adventist, supporting with the same arguments he did the biblical writings, the writings of Ellen White. His book argued that the Revised Version was, in part, a conspiracy against the one true church, which was his of course.[6] In this singular book is the genesis of the flood that gave us the babel which is the King James Only myth. It is also the first attempt at suggesting that the so-called Textus Receptus is the inspired text while the older manuscripts, generally

4 Oddly enough, one KJVO site 'examines' the Geneva Bible Only Cult. (http://www.blessedquietness.com/journal/housechu/kingjamesbibledefense.htm)

5 According to David Daniell, the KJV New Testament is between 80 and 90% of the Tyndale New Testament. The portions of the Old Testament which Tyndale was able to complete is similarly used by the 'translators' of the KJV.

6 This was on the basis of two key changes between the KJV and the RV; Acts 13.42 and Hebrews 9.27. (See *One Bible Only? Examining Exclusive Claims for the King James Bible* by Roy E Beacham and Kevin T Bauder general editors (Kregel Publications: Grand Rapids 2001)

more recently discovered, were perverted tools of the devil. His prime arguments are against change, insisting that the motives of the RV committee were nothing more than a conspiratorial effort to rid the world of Protestantism in favor of Catholicism. We will spend some time with some of his more mythical arguments so as to see how they were developed by later KJVO apologists, while we try to ignore his more outlandish bigoted statements.

His first attack is that the RV (which by 1930 was fifty years old) lessened the degree of the miraculous. He suggests that the RV reading of eclipse of the sun which is present at the crucifix-ion is ordinary compared the KJV's reading of "and the sun was darkened." There is no turning to the Greek and making use of lexical tools in his argument; he suggests only that higher critics have turned against miracles and thus the Revised Version renders passages without miracles (Wilkinson, 4-5). This is rampant in modern KJVO apologetics as well. Will Kinney suggests that the deity of Christ is under attack (a key refrain in all KJVO circles) in modern versions, such as at Acts 20.28. In each change, it is not due to Greek texts, or lower criticism, but to the devaluation of some sort of Christian belief. For Wilkinson in this instance, it was the miraculous. For Kinney, the change in Acts 20.28 was not based on any textual reading in reality, but a result of a long line of conspiracies to eradicate something or the other of Christianity.[7]

In a series entitled "The NIV, NASB, ESV, NET and other Vatican Versions reject the Hebrew Texts," Kinney shows his reli-ance upon the Hebrew texts.[8] Wilkinson suggests that the Hebrew Scriptures were always preserved. He writes without evidence, "By the time of Christ, the Old Testament was in a settled condition. Since then, the Hebrew Scriptures had been carried down intact to the day of printing (about 1450 A.D.) by the unrivalled methods of the Jews in transmitting perfect Hebrew manuscripts." (Wilkinson, 5) With no evidence provided, Kinney makes a similar statement, "The Hebrew Masoretic scribes were used of God to preserve His

---

7   http://brandplucked.webs.com/acts2028godsblood.htm
8   http://brandplucked.webs.com/nivnasbrejecthebrew.htm

inspired words in the Old Testament. Of the Bible versions widely used today in the English language, only the King James Bible consistently sticks to the Hebrew text." He also suggests that there is indeed no Samaritan Pentateuch or even a Septuagint, "The KJB is right and the fake bible versions are wrong for rejecting the Hebrew texts and following some fanciful Samaritan Pentateuch or the alleged Septuagint." Wilkinson suggests that all of these conspiracies to change the text by creating false manuscripts can be traced back to the Catholic Church (Wilkinson, 6). Kinney suggest the same.[9] Both men suggest that there are in reality only two bibles, the King James and the Catholic Bibles.[10]

The most enduring myth of Wilkinson which supports his assertion of the KJVO is the so-called Pure Bible of the Waldenses.[11] Again with no evidence, Wilkinson sets out various denominations which battled Rome, including the defenders of the Textus Receptus. He writes of these people, "the defenders of the Textus Receptus were of the humbler class who earnestly sought to follow the early church." Everyone else, or rather, the Catholic Church, bent the knee to Constantine who had been influenced, somehow, by Origen. To support his theory of a pure text, he created an underground network of defenders who thrived from Judea to Great Britain In fact, Great Britain, according to Wilkinson, was the center of a sect who followed the early Church until they were wiped out by Rome using the hands of the pagan Anglo-Saxons. Even with the paradigm shifts between Constantine and the Waldensian massacre, they were able to hold the pure bible of the early church secured from Judea. He writes, "It is held that the pre-Waldensian Christians of northern Italy could not have had doctrines purer than Rome unless their Bible was purer than Rome's; that is, was not of Rome's falsified manuscripts." (Wilkinson, 20) According to

---

9 http://brandplucked.webs.com/whoreofbabyloncatholic.htm
10 Wilkinson had only the RV to really challenge the KJV for the heart and mind of Protestantism while Kinney today spends all of his time attempting to destroy all other translations.
11 This consumes the entire second chapter of Wilkinson's book

Wilkinson, the Waldensian Church had been formed in 120 and had carried the pure text in a fight against Rome until it was able to hand it off to Luther. Luther was succeeded by Tyndale but it was the Jesuits who issued a bible in 1582 in a great conspiracy to destroy Protestantism.

Wilkinson begins his chapter on the birth of the King James in a very grandiose and jingoistic manner. "The hour had arrived," Wilkinson writes, "and from the human point of view, conditions were perfect, for God to bring forth a translation of the Bible which would sum up in itself the best of the ages." (Wilkinson, 16) What was the time? The English language had ripened to maturity, the scholarship on both the Hebrew and the Greek materials had been perfected, but beyond this, it was the birth of the British Empire which he connects to the "great American Republic" that would spread the pure Word of God across the globe. We can find much the same reasons in modern KJVO apologetics as well. However, of importance is Wilkinson's insistence that the merger of the cosmic events which seemly only happened once was a divine sign that the KJV was the pure Word of God. Not only that, but it had come forward after the English had defeated the Jesuits in 1582 and had come at the request of "a thousand ministers" (Wilkinson, 19). These ministers were as far different from ministers of the Seventh-day Adventist Church, as they were from the Puritans.

Wilkinson supposes that not only had the English language reached perfection, but so too had scholarship, especially in the realm of the Textus Receptus. He cites numerous objections to the critical Greek Text prepared by Wescott and Hort and boldly states that the Received Text is the pure text which had travelled the centuries to land upon the desk of the English scribes. It was not only the Hebrew and Greek manuscripts which had been infallibly preserved, but the translators themselves. Paying no attention to any of the English Bibles which proceeded the KJV, Wilkinson supposed that these men were nothing less than inspired, missing the great irony of the legend of the Letter of Aristeas and how such legends usually developed around mythical books. He concludes his chapter on the King James itself by citing the prose of it, which one cannot easily argue against, but again, missing the borrowed beauty from Tyndale (and other versions) that preceded the KJV.[12]

Wilkinson believed that the KJV followed the Received Text, something that had flowed from the Apostles, vouchsafed from centuries of Catholic attacks, and finally delivered to the greatest of all peoples, the English, so that the world could be subjected to Christ. Yet, no real trace of the Textus Receptus can be found. This has played no small part in many leaving the King James Only position and traveling just a hair to the left to the Textus Receptus Only position as advocated by the Trinitarian Bible Society. They go so far as to dare to suggest that the words of the translators are uninspired but should always be based on the Textus Receptus. This "confession" has done little to comfort men like Will Kinney who calls it "meaningless." Kinney knows that there is no such thing as the Textus Receptus. He acknowledges that editions of the Received Text reverse translated from the KJV to fill in missing places. Indeed, he declares, "Their TR did not give rise to the KJB but it was the KJB that gave rise to their printed copies of their Textus Receptus!" He also writes, "If God chose the KJB translators to give us His pure and complete Greek text, then He logically and consistently also gave them spiritual insight and divine direction on HOW these same texts were to be translated into the English tongue."[13]

He and others do not simply stop there but go further. Kinney suggests that the KJV corrects the Hebrew and the Greek. "I believe God guided the KJB translators not only to the correct underlying Hebrew and Greek texts (after all, only God knows for sure what He inspired to be put in His book) but also guided them as to the

---

12 The King James' Translators, in their note to the readers, claimed revision, but not pure translation, "Zeale to promote the common good, whether it be by devising any thing our selves, or revising that which hath bene laboured by others, deserveth certainly much respect and esteeme, but yet findeth but cold intertainment in the world."
13 http://brandplucked.webs.com/tyntrorkjb.htm

best possible meaning in the English language."[14] Kinney is not alone in this belief. Peter Ruckman, a Baptist pastor in northern Florida has gone so far as to suggest that the King James translators had an advanced revelation, even more than the revelation many believe the original authors have.[15] "Where the perverse Greek reads one way and the A.V. reads the other, rest assured that God will judge you at the Judgment on what you know. Since you don't know the Greek (and those who knew it, altered it to suit themselves), you better go by the A.V. 1611 text" (Ruckman, 126). Gail Riplinger similarly writes, "There existed a true original Greek (i.e. Majority Text, Textus Receptus). It is not in print and never will be because it is unnecessary. No one on the planet speaks first century Koine Greek, so God is finished with it. He needs no 'Dead Bible Society' to translate it into 'everyday English'"[16] (Riplinger, 956).

As the narrowing down of the "infallible Word of God" camp arrives at a razor thin point, it has become miniscule with the eruption of a group promoting what they call the Cambridge Pure Text Edition. As it stands today, there are two main KJV texts. One is the 1769 Oxford while the other is the Cambridge text. It differs by three words. They are found in Jeremiah 34.16, 2 Chronicles 33:19 and Nahum 3.16. There is also a controversy about this with some KJVO advocates failing to make a choice.[17] When pressed, Kinney can only offer that if it really matters, go with the Cambridge, "The King James Bible believer, when asked by others where we can get God's complete, inspired and 100% historically true words of God

---

14 http://brandplucked.webs.com/elevateenglishinsults.htm

15 Ruckman is another source of hypocrisy in the KJVO movement of generally strictly conservative Christians. He has had several divorces and in all fairness to other, more temperate KJV Defenders, is often rash and verbally abusive.

16 Riplinger's first book, *New Age Bible Versions: An Exhaustive Documentation of the Message, Men & Manuscripts Moving Mankind to the Antichrist's One World Religions* (A.V. Publications, 1993) made her a key figure in the debate.

17 http://www.kjv-only.com/rick/waites3errors.html

can confidently say that God's pure words of truth are found in any King James Bible you can buy in the stores today. If you are still hung up on the "ye" or "he" thingy in Jeremiah 34:16, then go with the Cambridge printings of the King James Holy Bible."[18] But, this is not the Pure Text camp. Instead, the Pure Text camp seeks a return to the old English spellings and orthography.[19] This camp is rather small, but it is the necessary and final conclusion to the idea of a pure text. After all, if as the KJVO proponents have us believe in connecting jots and tittles to the KJV, then the odd 'u' of the English spelling should likely be reserved.[20]

Jerome met with resistance when he first sought to bring the West into the use of Hebrew. Resistance died out. So did his translation. In the English West, the King James became the standard which achieved even more of a divine status than the Vulgate (and the Septuagint) before it. It too is dying out with the great majority of Christians using modern bibles. With the plethora of bible translations comes the sense that reading the bible has been somehow democratized. As with any paradigm shift, this causes the powers that be to seek a path forward that essentially keeps them in control. John Piper and translators like Leland Ryken have come to the forefront of the battle to decide which bible is best for the English speaking peoples. They have chosen the English Standard Version (Crossway, 2007). Piper has stated that he "would like to see the English Standard Version become the most common Bible of the English-speaking church, for preaching, teaching, memorizing, and study."[21] According to Ryken, one can trust the ESV because

---

18 http://brandplucked.webs.com/answerwhitewhichkjb.htm

19 http://www.bibleprotector.com/

20 http://www.biblebelievers.com/believers-org/counterfeit-jv.html. This is but one of the groups promoting the idea that Savior instead of Saviour demotes the deity of Christ and makes way for a Catholic takeover of the world. While these groups have not found each other yet, no doubt they will in the future.

21 http://www.desiringgod.org/resource-library/articles/good-english-with-minimal-translation-why-bethlehem-uses-the-esv

"it adheres to the right translation philosophy." This theory is his own pet theory, the "essentially literal translation" philosophy as opposed to the dynamic equivalent translation (DE) found in such bibles as the New Living Translation (Tyndale, 2007). In both a book and an online published paper, Ryken argues forcefully against DE translations.[22] More to the point, he argues that DE translations are less theologically precise, with many of them no longer using the word, or the forms of the word, justification. This theological preciseness is most evident in the use of the ESV (as opposed to other gender inclusive versions) when one examines Ryken and Piper along with Wayne Grudem, who hold to a rather Reformed (complementarian) view of women in the ministry.[23] This suggestion of theological preciseness, especially when it comes to the role of women in the Church is not the first time that it has prompted a bible translation.

The Millenary Petition of 1604 was the petition which Wilkinson suggested 1,000 Puritan ministers signed. It contained several points of concern which concern about the state of the Anglican Church at the turn of the 17th century. These concerns were generally Protestant in number, but an unusual one for the time is one which unites the rise of the ESV as a dominate force in the Reformed Church and the call for the KJV. It involves the administration of the sacrament of baptism by women followed immediately by the suggestion that only men, albeit well-qualified men, be admitted to the ministry.[24] The original has been lost, but a replication from 1655 remains, which reads in part, "Our humble suit, then, unto your majesty is that these offences following, some may be removed, some amended, some qualified: baptism not to be ministered by women, and so explained .... Concerning Church ministers: that none hereafter be admitted into the ministry but

---

22 http://www.harvestdavenport.org/content/10198/88983.pdf

23 http://www.bbc.edu/journal/volume8_2/esv_review.pdf

24 Encyclopædia Britannica Online, s. v. "Millenary Petition", accessed May 25, 2012, http://www.britannica.com/EBchecked/topic/382718/Millenary-Petition.

able and sufficient men, and those to preach diligently and especially upon the Lord's day." We must note that the trumpeters of the
ESV often cite the gender-neutral approach of other translations
as reason why the ESV is superior.[25]

Our love of fate as a species is evident in our mythology. The
idea of eternal recurrence in ancient mythology serves us well to
define why we continue to repeat the same mistakes, and often for
the same reasons, as we have in the past. Jerome faced the Septu-
agintal loyalists. Tyndale faced the whole of the Catholic Church,
dying to win. The modern versions have all but unseated the King
James Version mirroring a paradigm shift between worlds (First and
Third). Time marches on, but we continue to march in circles. The
King James Version Only movement is one which lurks in our fears
of change. It is a species of thought no different than Creationist
theology or the oppressive rules which refuse an equal standing with
women. While it suffers a quiet death on the internet, the rise of the
English Standard Version as the dominant (or rather, the hoped for
dominant) translation is not far behind it. What causes these odd-
ities? No doubt, Protestantism as a whole contributes to the often
divergent views from which emerge power-grabbing movements.
Yet, Protestantism only provides the room for these shoots to grow.

The King James Version of the bible came about when the
Puritans, the more conservative members of the Anglican Church,
saw what they considered a deplorable condition. For them, the
Church was too Catholic and had allowed women to administer,
at the very least, baptism. King James saw an opportunity to rid
himself of the margin notes of the Geneva Bible which continu-
ously challenged his authority. At the start of the Great Depression,
long after World War I (significant for the Seventh-day Adventist),
Wilkinson was facing a serious change in society if not his church.
He was a contender for a stricter view on the inerrancy of Scripture

25 For example, see Kevin DeYoung's pamphlet on why his church
switched to the ESV (Crossway, 2011) http://static.crossway.org/
excerpt/why-our-church-switched-to-the-esv/why-our-church-
switched-to-the-esv.pdf

(and Ellen White's teachings). How better to secure such a sentiment than to suggest that it was not just the original languages which were inspired, but now too the English version. Faced with the advent of scholarship and archeological discoveries, new bibles were being printed which, mixing with the rise of Communism, the rise of Evolution, and other social changes, fundamentalists retreated further away from mainstream Protestantism allowing the KJVO movement to be fully born. They have sharpened their attack in recent decades, moving away from needing originals and from the Textus Receptus to suggesting that the KJV is so inspired, that it is advanced revelation. They often charge their opponents with virtual atheism or if the opponents are lucky, at the very least, apostasy. Anti-Catholic bigotry and conspiracy theories abound in the KJVO camp.

What I have not covered is the psychological attachment to the KJVO, and I do not intend to do so fully now as it is difficult to describe in detail why people choose so steadfastly to hold to the KJVO. In my personal experience, it is because "if it was good enough to save me" then it is still good enough to save anyone. Further, there are those who have based the entirety of their Christianity upon the KJV (much like some have with inerrancy), such as Will Kinney. For them, if the KJV is not the "100% Word of God," then there is none. While much of their doctrine is not explained, this point becomes almost circular, with their reasoning if one should inquire as to why one needs such a tool to simply point at such passages as Psalm 12.6-7 (something not used to describe any bible translation until 1930). Their attachment runs deep and is often unexplainable, but it is not different, really, that attachments developed to other facets of various beliefs.

The King James Version Only movement will last barely a generation more. It is long past its due time and is only being supported by the vast ranges of the internet which has an equal number of pages of challenges to the myth of the KJVO. It was built on fear and allowed to propagate only on fear of the worst sort. It has spawned a new movement which is slowly but surely taking shape, first with the literal equivalent movement and now what can only be termed the ESVO movement. Once these are done, it will be another translation, in another time, and in another place which people latch onto.

Works Consulted but not Cited

Barr, James, *Fundamentalism.* (Harrisburg: Trinity Pr Intl.) 1981

White, James, *King James Only Controversy, The: Can You Trust Modern Translations?* (Grand Rapids: Bethany House) 2009

Works Cited

Daniell, David, *The Bible in English.* (New Haven, CT: Yale University Press) 2003

Riplinger, Gail A., *In Awe of Thy Word,* (Ararat, Virginia: Authorized Version Publications, 2004)

Ruckman, Peter, *The Christian's Handbook of Manuscript Evidence* (Pensacola: Pensacola Bible Press, 1990)

Wilkinson, Benjamin G., *Our Authorized Bible Vindicated.* (2005)

5

From Tongues to Methods

Rev. Josheua E. Blanchard

My journey begins at large suburban Assemblies of God church in the suburbs of Detroit, Michigan. I was about 8 years old or so … my family was an itinerate church family. We tried several churches, Nazarene, Baptist, and even a Lutheran Church (WELS for those who are familiar with Lutheran denominations). We never fit anywhere as a family. My mother was a "dyed in the wool" Assemblies of God Pentecostal while my father was a cradle Methodist. None of the churches we attended as a family ever seemed to fit. We attended a large Baptist church for a while, and even became members, all so that my sisters and I could attend the Christian school there at a discounted tuition rate. After my oldest sister graduated we stopped going there too.

After the Baptist church we moved around sparingly, never really attending church, then when I was 8 I was accepted to Northville Christian School and was sent to the church's VBS, so that I could make friends. My memory of that week is vivid. I had a lot of fun and at the end of the week I gave my heart to Jesus after repeating the VBS leaders' version of the "sinner's prayer." I had a lot to be forgiven for, I spent my days as an 8 year old popping M&M's and drinking a fifth of Kool Aid and living in rebellion by not picking up my dirty underwear like my mother had told me to "at least 1000 times" (said in my mother stern voice). Despite the sarcasm, the moment was very formative and I began asking my parents if I could attend church and being the supportive people that they were and always have been, they took me faithfully every Sunday from that point on.

Like I said, that was just the start. I attended every Sunday and Wednesday. The School was at the church and the church was at the school so I was there everyday, seeing many of the same people five and six time a week until I out grew the school and had to attend the public High School. I listened and grew; I was baptized with water at age 10, and baptized in the Holy Spirit at age 11 (at summer camp) with the initial physical evidence of speaking in tongues. At 12 I went on a mission trip into Northern Michigan, not far from where I currently am appointed. It was there I received my call to what A/G folks refer to as "full-time ministry," and what mainliners call ordained ministry. I flirted with the idea of being a lawyer, a teacher, even a Physical therapist, but always came back to ordained ministry.

My adolescence is where I received my fundamentalist training. The Senior Pastor of the megachurch I attended was pretty healthy and even, by A/G standards, a moderate, but the youth Pastor was a different story. Pastor Mike was a genuine, serious, and zealous man. He fervently believed that without Christ the soul was damned and that without the Holy Spirit the Christian was lost. There is nothing wrong with these beliefs, I believe them myself, but it's not what he believed, it's how he believed it. Mike was a fanatic; he believed that everything had spiritual value, either good or bad. He didn't believe that there was a demon behind every bush, but two demons behind every bush. He believed that every illness, every vice, every behavior that did not fit his narrow interpretation of the bible was demonic. He was a disciple of the Toronto blessing, the Brownsville Revival and the Bogotá outpouring. He once convinced a friend of mine to stop taking his bi-polar meds, because it showed a lack of faith. As a result my friend tried to kill himself. Mike would regularly invite a group of demon hunters called, the "Hell Fighters" to our church to conduct services that would root out demonic and evil spirits within us. Under Mike's leadership I became a leader in the youth group.

I lead prayer meetings, preached at youth group meetings, taught Sunday school and lead revivals at my High School. I also became convinced that rated R movies were demonic, alcohol was demonic, tobacco was demonic, kissing girls was demonic, kissing boys was demonic, listening to the radio was demonic ... just about everything but praying and reading the bible was demonic. I threw away hundreds of dollars worth of CD's, ended friendship, even got in trouble at school (telling people they were going to hell was not a value of the Novi Community School District ... probably still isn't) all because I was convinced that God was a narrow minded and strict God that required absolute obedience, all, of course, within the guise of our narrow interpretation of scripture. At 19 I graduated form High School and left Mike's ministry to prepare for full-time ministry at Southwestern Assemblies of God University (SAGU) in Waxahachie, Texas. Things really began to change then.

I arrived at SAGU pious and holier than thou. I expected everyone to be there for the same reason I was, which was not the case. Some people were there to become businesswomen, teachers, and social workers, but to me, none of those things mattered. What mattered was the high calling of the preacher. After all, why stoop to be a peasant when God has called you to be a king? It didn't take long for my world to change. One of my very first classes was with a man named Dr. Paul Alexander. Paul was a young professor who taught the New Testament, Greek, Theology, and Ethics. His perspective was unlike any I had come across, he seemed to be a ... LIBERAL (really he was very moderate to conservative then, just not a fundie). Things really changed in the fall of 2001. I was in my early morning class, a hermeneutics class with an ass of a man named Donny Lutick. Class had just ended and I was tired. It was an 8:00am class. I went back to the dorm and entered the lobby to find 100 people around the TV. I began to watch and what I saw was a building in New York on fire, one of the Twin Towers. I watched for about anther 30 minutes and then careening across the sky came another plan ... BOOOM!! It slammed into the other tower!!! We all later learned that it was a terrorist attack. Eventually the towers fell and thousands died and America mourned, but not too long after she was firing up her war machine. At first I was like everyone else, I wanted war, I wanted blood, but in all that hate and anger and violence, some of which was proclaimed from pulpits and from the school's president, there was Dr. Paul, asking, "What would Jesus do?" It was from that moment that my fundie shell began to crack and peel.

I began seeking answers for why and how and Dr. Paul helped me see that God had nothing to do with the tragedy happening, but everything to do with those who suffered from it. The following semester I got married and my wife and I simply lost faith in the A/G and the fundamentalist worldview. We found refuge in the Episcopal Church. There we were confirmed, our sons were baptized and we found a faith that spoke to us, a faith with tangibles, such as sacraments, liturgy, and ordered prayer. It wasn't until we had been married for 7 years that I found United Methodism. I began attending the UMC because it provided a job and place to take my kids on Sunday. I worked part time as a Youth Director and full time as a social worker at a UM extension ministry called the Circle of Care. I grew to love the people called Methodist and this is how.

They loved me and my family without reserve: From the very first time we attend the First UMC of Sallisaw, Oklahoma, people were asking how can we help. We struggled financially during those times and every bit counted. They brought us clothes, food and even Christmas gifts. My wife delivered our 3rd son during that time and they cooked meals, called and even visited when no one else did. When we finally left the Circle of Care and moved to Sallisaw so I could work at the church and attend seminary, one of the old church ladies found out that we needed a refrigerator for our rental and she bought one and had it delivered!

They taught me about the grace and love of God; I have always felt unworthy before God, even as an Episcopalian I never felt like God and I were ok. The people called Methodist taught this little doctrine called assurance. That is the belief that as long as you have faith and have trust in God, no matter what, God forgives you. This was such a relief! I learned about sacraments and other means of grace (Bible study, prayer, fasting, and attending worship plus helping the needy) as ways we could draw near to God, but that God did not require them in exchange for his love.

They confirmed and provided a way for my call to ordained ministry: I had felt a call to ministry for so long, but the A/G was and is so nepotistic, I never found meaningful and gainful employment as an A/G minister. I had given up the call and was content with the idea that I would be a social worker my whole life (which is an honorable thing). The Methodist church mentored me, sent me to seminary, provided a home, a salary, health insurance and wonderful and God fearing leaders that served as my District Superintendents. All this has allowed me to flourish as a young pastor, to grow as a husband, father and Christian. I am now a seminary graduate approaching ordination and serving two wonderful churches and being supervised by one of the most compassionate and generous Superintendants one could ask for.

So why the transition, why did I leave fundamentalism? Because fundamentalism made no sense, fundamentalism is destructive, and fundamentalism is not good news. I have found within moderate Methodism a healthy, safe and fertile place, where the kingdom of God is. I have no doubt that had I not left fundamentalism when I did and had I not stumbled upon the people called Methodist, I'd have no faith to speak of. I value my Pentecostal up brining, I even still relate to Pentecostals well. I am a member of the Society for Pentecostal Studies as well as a member of the Wesleyan Theological Society. There is no love lost between Pentecostals and myself, but I am so glad to be a moderate Methodist!

6

A Journey into Faith

This light guided me more surely than the light of noonday To the place where he (well I knew who!) was awaiting me– A place where none appeared.

Rev. Anthony Buglass

I first rejected Christian faith at the age of 10. I had been sent to church with two of my younger brothers, and found it to be the most boring waste of Sunday afternoons imaginable. It was very traditional, with twee children's songs which even at that age took the enamel off my teeth, and a pretty literal telling of Bible stories. While I was being taught this religion in church, I met science for the first time at school. It made sense, and it was different from the religious explanations. I didn't know how to put them together, and didn't know how to ask my Sunday School teachers, so I felt I had to choose. Science was much more logical to my 10-year-old mind, so I decided there was no God: like the French mathematician Laplace (of whom I'd never heard), I had no need of that hypothesis. I still had to go to Sunday School, because my parents insisted I help my second brother get the youngest one there. To go through such tedium when you know it's pointless truly compounds the misery! So it was that when at the age of 12 they finally allowed me to stop, I made a vow never to darken the door of a church ever again. (Note to the reader – be very careful saying things like that: I reckon God heard, and that's when he decided he was going to call me to the ministry!)

I went through high school as an avowed atheist, studied a range of subjects including biology, accepted all the usual modernist assumptions about the world and how it happened, and never seriously considered the religious alternative. Then, in the summer of my 17th birthday, found myself pondering the possibility of God's existence. What I had learned through science revealed to me a world of dazzling complexity – surely it couldn't all be a co-incidence? There had to be Something behind it all – perhaps that's what people meant when they talked about 'God.' So I took the step of accepting the existence of God, but I had no intention of having anything to do with church: the memory of those blighted Sundays stayed with me, and I wasn't going back there again. However, when I went back to school for the new year, some friends whom I knew through a local youth choir had transferred to my school. They were Christians, and began telling me about some of the things they did in their church – they had a youth club, and a Sunday youth group, and monthly youth meetings with dances. And girls. Suddenly church sounded like an attractive possibility...

I began attending our little local chapel one dark November evening. I didn't know the preacher, didn't know the hymns, didn't know anybody apart from the friends who normally attended (but who weren't there that week), but for the first time in my life I really prayed. It just happened. I found myself addressing God in frank honesty: "I don't know if you're there or not, but if you are please show me, so I'm not wasting your time or mine looking in the wrong place." Funny sort of prayer, but all of a sudden I knew I was not alone. There was a Presence, as if he was standing behind my chair with his hand on my shoulder, quietly saying "It's all right, I am here – we've got some way to go yet, but we're going to go together." That was life-changing: I had no concept of a life journey or spiritual journey, this was a new idea, but I knew whatever happened I could never be an unbeliever again.

For the next year, I attended that little chapel every Sunday evening, walked on to our youth fellowship, went to the youth club and dances, flirted with the girls and got nowhere, and enjoyed being part of everything. Exactly a year after first joining, I went with them to a residential youth weekend: discussions, fun, a Saturday night dance – and God met me face to face. That is how it felt. My Damascus Road moment. After the last dance, we stopped where we were, got out the hymnbooks, and had our evening prayer together. I had volunteered to read the Bible reading, and it spoke to me. When I say it spoke to me, it grabbed me by the lapels and made me pay attention. When I finished, my friend began leading in prayer, and I didn't hear a word he said – it was as if that circle of a hundred or so teenagers simply faded away and there was just me and God, face to face in a pool of light. He gently invited me to let him in, the kind of invitation which made sense of that first thought of the journey together, the kind of invitation you can't refuse: It was as if the person you've always respected and fancied but thought was way out of your league suddenly said they were in love with you. I said "Yes." In that moment, I was flooded with light and peace, I was born again – my life changed. My call to preach came out of that moment, so much was different.

I tell the story in some detail, because that is the real core and foundation of my Christian faith. The group was a typical British Methodist youth group, in a typical Northern Methodist setting: more or less evangelical, but not especially fundamentalist. I answered the appeal and went forward to publicly commit my life to Christ in the next day's communion service, and was offered some counselling – mainly, to use some simple Bible study notes and take some time every day to read my Bible and pray. That was it. I was a young and immature 18, suddenly looking at my life and world through a very different lens. My family didn't share it: my father was a working-class labourer and atheist, my mother had been a Salvationist in her youth, but her faith had been overlaid by the years of care and poverty, and was a faint flame utterly obscured by the adolescent rows we were working through. She didn't recognise my faith, I didn't recognise hers. That came much later. As far as I was concerned, I was the only Christian in the house.

INTO FUNDAMENTALISM

The key moment in what came next was a challenge from a friend: "Do you believe the Bible is the Word of God?" I was a little taken aback, and muttered "Suppose ..." so he showed me 2 Timothy 3:16. Not to be outdone (I couldn't let him be a 'better Christian' than me ...) I said "I believe it!" That brought a powerful sense of affirmation: it was profoundly comforting for a young adolescent to find something so black-and-white, solid and secure as an expression of faith. I consciously adopted a strongly fundamentalist approach to the Bible. Now I knew what we were to believe and preach, I knew who was 'in' and who was 'out' – so many things came into focus for me. I rejected all I had learned about evolution and the scientific explanations for the origins of the universe – the only explanation that mattered was what the Bible taught. I was dimly aware of a slight niggle, an underlying discomfort which I couldn't put my finger on or put into words. I think it was what I later learned was cognitive dissonance: I was telling myself something was true, and something else was untrue, but I didn't understand why. My heart was trying to persuade my brain that evolution and stuff was wrong, while my brain was trying to say "But it makes sense..." and being told to shut up. I filed the discomfort alongside all the other discomforts of my turbulent life: we were a faithful remnant, standing against an unbelieving world and a liberal and apostate church – of course we were uncomfortable! I was also looking for the beginning of my life of ministry: I had to train as a local preacher before I could offer for ministry, and that meant I had to find work and get on with life at home for however long it would take. I desperately wanted to escape the prison of my town and housing estate – it was easy to hide all my discomforts in that yearning to be on the road serving my God.

There was another layer of discomfort: if any of my friends challenged or questioned the faith, I had to be able to give an answer. To say "I don't know" was tantamount to admitting that Christianity didn't work, and admitting defeat in the debate between faith and unbelief. I had no problem with arguing, because I was very keen to witness and bring people to faith – my discomfort was because I actually knew very little. I had a very limited and shallow understanding of the Bible, no understanding of Christian doctrine, and a very patchy understanding of how the different questions related to each other. Of course, I couldn't admit that: I was a very adolescent 19-year-old, and desperate not to reveal my weaknesses to those who would use them to overturn the faith to which I was profoundly committed.

It must have been very difficult for the wiser heads who were trying to guide and nurture me. I still remember a session with our minister discussing Methodist beginnings, in which he had said something about what Wesley believed, and which seemed to me to contradict clear biblical teaching, and I exploded "Then John Wesley was a heretic!" Oh, the arrogance of youth! I am sure that very ordinary middle-of-the-road minister must have prayed a great deal for his very earnest youth group!

Our group wasn't the only one: there was a network of four or five fellowships connected to the local Methodist churches, all fairly evangelical, increasingly charismatic, but with differing emphases. One of the other groups began to develop its own leadership, and became increasingly dogmatic and strict. They regarded their minister as very liberal, so they had little to do with him. They began reading the works of Dr Martyn Lloyd Jones, and from there they stepped into the writings of John Calvin. Their dogmatic stance led to certain practices which felt very hard-line to the rest of us: one young girl had been given a silver crucifix for her birthday, and the leaders took exception to this. She was told that she should be wearing an empty cross, because the crucifix by implication denied the resurrection. She objected, and was 'disciplined' – she was excluded from the fellowship until she showed them the cross with the Christ-figure removed. Because so many of her friends were part of the group, she felt unable to disengage, so bowed to the pressure and did as she was asked. That episode left a bad taste among us. Their arguments all sounded very good and very scriptural, and were quoted with great authority and backed up by "the Doctor" (Lloyd Jones) or Calvin. However, I was increasingly aware of a legalism which felt wrong, somehow. I couldn't tell the difference between the way they were using the Bible and the way the Pharisees had used the Law; I was sure there must be a difference, or that would make us Pharisees, but I couldn't tell what that difference could be.

There were lots of good things happening during those years. My faith was real, and growing, and there was a real dynamism among our crowd of very active Christian young people. Charismatic renewal exploded on the scene, with a number of big 'Days of Renewal' – these were exciting times for young Christians! There was a lot of speculation about the Second Coming, especially when the 1973 Yom Kippur War broke out, and all the Christian magazines were full of articles about how this was the beginning of the End, fulfilling all sorts of scriptures. Now, part of me was very excited about this: to be one of the blessed generation who would actually see the Second Coming was quite a thought. However, I had just met a lovely young lady, and we were very much in love, and part of me was hoping that there would be time before the End for our relationship to blossom and flourish, and get as far as marriage. The other part of me was feeling a bit guilty that there was any part of me hoping that the Second Coming would delay, either because I didn't want to be 'raptured' as a virgin, or because (to be honest) it was all a bit too big to handle – I was actually quite happy with the prospect of an 'ordinary' life of faith. All of this fed the undercurrent of discomfort, raising questions which I couldn't really shape about what I really believed – and questions which would almost certainly incur the displeasure of others in the fellowships.

However, bigger changes were on the horizon for me, with their own particular blend of promise and threat: I was about to begin college training, in preparation for ministry.

THE THREAT AND PROMISE OF KNOWLEDGE

British Methodism has a particular pathway for those who feel called to ministry. First, it is necessary to become a Local Preacher, which is a lay office – an unpaid volunteer who travels around the circuit at the direction of the superintendent minister taking services. That means taking certain courses and exams in order to qualify. After that, it is necessary to go through a process of committees and interviews, before Conference accepts the offer and the student is sent to college to train for ordination.

I had begun my Local Preacher training by the usual methods, studying at home tutored by my minister. The first course I did was largely to do with the preparation and leading of worship, and I hadn't got as far as the biblical or doctrinal courses. I had decided to go to Bible college for a year, doing a course which would get me through those subjects more quickly than doing it all at home, and setting me up for the later college course. Cliff College is a Methodist and evangelical Bible college in Derbyshire, UK. In those days, it offered a one-year course, encompassing biblical study, doctrine, evangelism and counselling courses, all grounded in the practice of student missions and preaching. It was residential, so students lived together in a Christian community with all the blessings and tensions that caused.

I was excited about being a Cliff student, but also more than a bit nervous. I felt I could trust Cliff because it was evangelical: the whole course was designed to help us understand and share the word of God. I was also a bit older, and beginning to leave behind that adolescent need to see things in black and white; I was aware that there were grey areas between the certainties, and it didn't necessarily mean failure if I had to say "I don't know." It just meant I still had time to find out!

I loved my year at Cliff. I loved most of all that for the first time, I began to understand the Bible. Up to then, I was beginning to know my way round, and knew where to find the stories or texts I wanted. However, there were acres of Old Testament which I didn't know, and the OT prophetic books were really no more than places to find texts which proved that Jesus was the Messiah. Now, for the first time, I began to understand how to read the books in their historical contexts. It was a relatively superficial understanding, compared to what I would learn later at university, but it was enough to draw a different sketch-map of what the Bible meant. Our theology course was very much a 'biblical theology' course, and was very evangelical in its structure and use of the texts – we knew that there were other 'wrong' theologies in the church: 'liberal' and 'radical' were dirty words, and we knew the names of those whose writings were not to be trusted. (What that really means is that there were certain names who symbolised all that we knew was wrong – we didn't study them, we didn't begin to understand them: we just knew they weren't 'biblical' or 'sound' so they had to be wrong.)

My year at Cliff dispelled a lot of the underlying discomforts I had felt, because I was no longer trying to reconcile opposites. Science was no longer a problem, because I was happy to see evolution as part of the process of creation. I had left behind the fundamentalism which needed to hold to a 6,000-year-old creation. There was a strong emphasis on traditional Methodist understandings of sanctification and holiness, which helped me to come to terms with the questions raised by the differences between what the Bible said about being Christian and my personal experiences of failing to be all that I should be. I felt as if a lot of shadows were dispelled, as if I'd been born again in the woods and had been following a narrow path through the trees, and had now come to the edge of the forest to see the foothills of the holy mountain itself reaching up before me and the light of the holy city on top beckoning me on into the climb. That became a running image for me, a metaphor of my spiritual journey: I could see steep climbs ahead, those places which look as if you're about to reach the summit, but when you get there it's still a long way ahead. Most importantly, I knew I was to climb in the company of my Guide.

I returned home from Cliff to go through the year-long process of offering for ministry. I took with me not only a much better and more systematic understanding of the faith, but the experience of engaging in mission and evangelism, open-air preaching, life in a Christian community. I returned to see that changes were happening there, too. Some of the Methodist fellowships had broken away to become schismatic independent house churches. Most of them were driven by charismatic renewal, and unwilling to remain a church set-up where they were not allowed to exercise the charismata in Sunday worship, or forced to work under the leadership of clergy they considered not Spirit-filled. The increasingly Calvinist group had decided the whole Methodist Church was unsound and apostate, and had migrated more or less en masse to a Calvinist free church some miles away. The situation had changed, both for me and for them. Instead of being an insecure and threatened adolescent in a dark and narrow place, I was much more confident and poised on a sunlit outcrop ready to embark on a major climb.

ONWARD AND UPWARD

Cliff was a safe place to face the threat of knowledge: it was a Christian college. Although I knew I'd be living in a Methodist theological college and would have the support of that Christian community, I knew that most of my studying would be done in a secular university. This would be the biggest challenge I would yet face. I tried to prepare for university by reading books by authors whose names had been symbols of liberal heresy, and that was one of the biggest surprises I had yet found: while there were points at which I knew I couldn't agree with them, I could see what they were trying to say, and found I agreed with it. Suddenly, the whole theological landscape was different: instead of a clear map, beyond which were the badlands inhabited by heretical dragons, I could now see different paths through the unknown territories. Some were better than others, but all of them showed a way through.

I began my training, and my degree studies, with a combination of excitement and fear. There were Christians in the theology department as well as the college, so I wasn't lacking spiritual support and fellowship, but the road ahead was increasingly open. About a month into my first term, I began to feel an intriguing combination of uncertainty and faith. The metaphor of the mountain came to mind: I knew I was climbing, roped to my Guide. I had always been able to see where I'd come from, and sometimes where I was hoping to reach, but things were beginning to change. It felt as if I could no longer be certain of where I'd been, or where I was going. It was like climbing a vertical face and entering a cloud: I could no longer see up or down, the only things which were certain were that I was on this cliff-face, and that I was still roped to my Guide. All the usual things – the mental theological structure which I'd had since Cliff, the perspective of my testimony and spiritual experience of being born again and filled with the Spirit – all faded into uncertainty, and I was no longer certain of anything but the climb and the Guide. It was a profound experience, lasting several weeks and even months. I discussed it with friends and fellow students, and continued on the journey. It was never enough of a crisis to make me wonder why I was still there, or consider resigning from training: on the contrary, it was as if I was being weaned from a faith in evangelical Christianity and into a faith in God. It was scary, and exciting. In time, the clouds seemed to clear, and many of the old certainties returned, but not as clearly as they once had been. The critical scholarship to which I was now exposed was no doubt having an effect on my spirituality, but it was far from negative. It felt as if I was shaking off things which were unnecessary, focusing more on what was necessary – as any climber must do, to lighten the load and free himself for the climb ahead.

Over the next three years, I studied biblical texts in Greek and Hebrew, philosophy and moral philosophy, Indian and African religions, 19th and 20th century church history and thought, early church history and biblical tradition and archeology. On the one hand, it made me all the more aware of the ways in which God has been active in history (so many stories to tell and retell!), on the other it exposed the weaknesses in the simple dogmatic assertions which had been part of the package of faith and belief which the church had given me. I was preaching and involved in local churches all through the process, and felt as if I were juggling between the questions which I wanted to explore and the certainties and simplicities of ordinary church life. It continued into my year as a probationer minister, and eventually focussed on the meeting at which I had to make the official affirmations in order to be recommended for ordination at the following Conference. By this time, I had been working as a minister for several months, preaching, teaching, in pastoral charge, conducting weddings and funerals, and it felt so right: this was clearly what I was called to do, and what God wanted me to do. There was a niggle, however, which wouldn't go away. It focused in this case on the Trinity. In order to be recommended for ordination, I had to affirm that I accepted and would "preach our doctrines" – and I wasn't sure how I would answer that question. Having studied both early church history and theology, I really wasn't happy with affirming the Nicene Creed or the Trinity as definitive statements of faith. I had seen too much of the political machinations which led to the formulations of the statements, and I was increasingly out of tune with the philosophical assumptions of the Greek and Latin Fathers who had written these statements. How could I affirm words which I thought needed at least three levels of translation before they made sense? On the other hand, how could I say 'no' and walk away from that which I had spent about 8 years building, including career and home?

I went to the synod meeting that morning, still wondering what I should do. I hadn't discussed it with anyone, because in my heart of hearts I knew I'd say 'yes' when asked if I preached our doctrines, but I was still working out why. It came to me as I sat with the other ordinands and prepared to step forward and face the questions: never mind the actual words, I did believe what they were trying to say. The Fathers and I faced the same mystery, and in our ways tried to articulate our response to it. I might have huge problems with Trinitarian language about hypostases and things, but however I tried to work it out, I knew that I believed in one God who was Father, Son and Holy Spirit. It occurred to me that God was saying "Never mind them – trust me." I did. When I was asked the question "Do you believe and preach our doctrines?" I answered "Yes" – and felt from deep within such a well of affirmation, that I knew it was the Spirit witnessing with my spirit. There is something profoundly powerful about looking to God and saying "Yes."

THE JOURNEY CONTINUES.

The events I described above are now three decades ago. I did affirm and was ordained. I have spent the last three decades serving in ministry in various places in the North of England, including not only pastoral care of churches but chaplaincy in prison, hospital and RAF. I have found myself ministering to people of all faiths and none, working in many different contexts – music festivals, schools, weddings, funerals, baptisms. I have felt the presence of God in places I would never have dreamt of going in my early years – as when I found myself conducting a Methodist baptismal service, to discover just beforehand that the family had chosen a Jewish lesbian godmother. I did the service anyway, thinking it was easier to let God sort out the implications, as a result of which I had an email a few weeks later from her teenage son asking if I would do his bar mitzvah. A Methodist minister, doing a bar mitzvah, for the non-practising Jewish son of a Jewish lesbian? Sometimes I wonder if God is having a laugh .... But how else do we connect with people and share faith, if we're not ready to go where they are? And if that raises questions about what we believe, hiding behind a wall of prooftexts is no way to engage with the truth.

What effect has all of this had on my personal beliefs? In one sense I feel that I believe fewer things, but what I believe I believe more strongly. I have become more aware that some beliefs are central to the Christian faith, others are less so, and others are entirely

peripheral. Some of the long and passionate arguments I had decades ago about particular points of doctrine now seem so irrelevant
to the reality of living the Christian faith, and so incidental to our
understanding of God – back then they looked so important! But
the faith that I have found in God himself, in the One who came
to us in Christ – that is more focussed, more strong and shining
than ever. Walking with him is such an adventure, such a journey
into the unknown. And so full of promise.

On Reflection

How did I get to be here? My 20-year-old self would be utterly
horrified to hear my nearly-60-year-old self: he would have written
me off as some sort of heretic. But I'm not, far from it. Indeed,
as a minister and preacher, I am more and more excited at what I
will preach on Sunday to my congregations. Whatever my younger
self might have believed or expected, I truly believe that I do now
have a deeper grasp of the truth in my faith than ever before. And
because I am a lot older, I think I understand myself better than
I did. So, some reflections and conclusions on the significance of
my journey of faith:

» I needed to grow up. My 18-20-year-old self was a very
insecure, black-and-white adolescent. I needed a faith which
gave me a secure grasp on my world, which was suddenly
beginning to change. Faith is always a good and secure handle
to grab, but it doesn't bring secure answers with it. I needed to
find faith in God, but he is too big to understand. I needed to
find faith in Christ, but he is too enigmatic to understand. So
I found faith in the Bible, and more specifically in a particular
interpretation of the Bible. Anything which challenged that
understanding had to be rejected, shown to be wrong – the
alternative was that everything on which I based my life was
in jeopardy. As I grew a little older and more secure in who
I was, I realised that it wasn't such a disaster to say "I don't

know." God knows, whether or not I do. Perhaps I might find out this side of eternity, perhaps not. That would have been an issue to my 18-year-old self; it isn't now.

» I needed to escape. I felt trapped in that enclosed Northern estate. The visions of ministry and preaching felt like a lifetime away, and everything seemed so slow in developing. Eventually it happened: through my year at Cliff I was introduced to a wider Christian world, and through my training for ordination the horizons broadened further. I travelled to the opposite end of the country, and found a culture and a world very different to that in which I'd grown up. More to the point, they didn't know me, didn't remember the long-haired teenager who had taken such a dogmatic stance on issues nobody really understood. When I returned to the North-East, it was as a young minister, a professional with a wife and (soon) a family. I was no longer trapped by my past – on the contrary, because I spoke with a local accent, I was accepted as one of them, and my past became an asset rather than a hindrance.

» I needed to understand the Bible. I thought I did, and that's why I wanted to study it, but the more I studied the more I was aware that I hadn't really grasped it. So I studied Greek and Hebrew, spent time unpacking the history of the texts, and history behind the texts. I began to hear the voices of the biblical writers, rather than the voice I wanted to impose upon their writings. Instead of saying "the Bible says ..." I began to say "Isaiah says ..." or "Mark says ...". When the different voices began to clash, as inevitably happened when pre-Christian (OT) and Christian (NT) texts were set alongside each other, I began to hear the 'biblical symphony' – if you listen to an orchestra playing a symphony it's a wonderful sound; if you try to follow in the score, you find all kinds of different voices and different parts, but they do come together to create the whole chorus. And what a chorus it makes! Each of the parts is wonderful, and together they create a marvellous symphony of revelation and promise. They don't necessarily agree, just as the instruments of the orchestra can play in different voices, but out of their dissonance comes something utterly harmonious – the voice of God, addressing his people, heard in different places and interpreted by different minds, but combining into something which challenges, promises and enables as it envisions. So, when I read the Bible, and I am required to say "This is the Word of the Lord..." I'm pretty sure I'm not always affirming what others want to affirm by that – but so what? I do believe that God does speak through the Bible, through the many writers in their own centuries and the many hearers in our own.

» I needed to understand that I don't understand. That probably sounds a bit odd, but I was bumping up against the limits of theology and indeed of language, and needed to be able to reach beyond those limits. God is beyond our language, so if we try to hang on to definitions which try to contain him, we've got it wrong. The problems I mentioned with the Trinity are a good example: the more I studied the arguments of the Fathers, and wrestled with discussions of "one God in three Persons" the more uncomfortable I became. I didn't get it. It felt wrong. It was wrong, because translating the Greek hypostasis or the Latin persona as 'person' was very misleading – it was too easy to slide into tritheism. It was all tied up in the language of 4th century Neoplatonist, and I'm not a 4th century Neoplatonist (I can just about spell it, but that's it...) Of course, I was also aware that someone had said it is impossible to preach on the Trinity without sliding into some sort of heresy! It occurred to me that the real problem is that the doctrines were trying to define God, to contain him in a conceptual box. That reminded me of a Tom and Jerry cartoon, in which Tom is chasing Jerry around a bowling alley – Jerry dives into a ball through the finger-holes, Tom arrives, whips off his scarf and ties it round the ball, but hasn't a free finger to put on the half-knot so he can tie the second half. Up pops Jerry from somewhere and puts his finger on the knot, Tom ties it off, waves his thanks, then does the eye-popping double-take and the chase is on again. I felt we were trying to do to God what Tom was trying to do with Jerry, and Jerry was doing what God does: just when you think you've contained him in a neat doctrinal box, he pops up where you didn't expect him. I realised that the Trinity isn't a formula for containing the mystery, but a handle on the mystery of God, a window through which to look into something much bigger than our words could ever contain. I do believe what the Trinity is trying to say, but I don't think it is able to say it. That is true for a great deal of our theology: language has limits, but God doesn't.

» I needed to belong. For a young person who is not part of the 'in crowd' life can be a bit lonely. I wasn't good at sport, I didn't have the money or freedom to go out with a group of friends, it all felt a bit empty. When I became a Christian, I knew I belonged to something much bigger than myself. More to the point, in those early years I knew who were 'us' (those who believed and thought like me) and who were 'them' (unbelievers, other more liberal church members) – because they didn't believe as I did, that reinforced the conviction that I was right and they were wrong, and possibly not really Christians. That pushed me even more firmly into the camp to which I felt I belonged. As I moved on, through Bible college and training, I became more secure in who I was, and didn't need such a hard-line boundary of support behind which to hide. I discovered that many of those whom I had dismissed were in fact good and faithful believers. I discovered that many people who were not Christians were nevertheless good people whom it was worth knowing, people who often shared my goals even if they didn't share the reasons why we aimed for them. I still need to belong, but I feel I belong to a much bigger and more diverse and wonderful church than I was able to recognize before – a fellowship which enables rather than entraps. I belong to the human race. I belong to God.

Perhaps that final comment is the key. My journey of faith has brought me to the point where I feel I belong to God – I have faith in God, which is not the same as faith in the Bible, or faith in a particular doctrinal stance. Some of my beliefs have changed along the way, often because I have met them embodied in people: it is one thing to say that a divorcee ought not be allowed to marry in church, because the Bible says that would be sanctifying adultery, quite another when the divorcee is sitting in your study confessing the failure of the earlier relationship and the hope for a new start. It is one thing to say that the Bible condemns homosexual practices, quite another to meet dedicated and faithful gay Christians in committed and loving relationships. Some of those with whom I have fellowshipped in years gone by have disagreed with me, rejecting my views just as my 20-year-old self would have done, offering to pray for me (for which I always say thanks – I accept all the prayers I can get!). Others have found themselves on a similar journey, learning more about God, about the Bible, and about themselves as we travel together in faith. There is a common belief that once you abandon the certainties of 'sound biblical theology' you're on a slippery slope to heresy, unbelief, and even Hell. To be fair, I have met plenty of people who have abandoned the faith, but few of them have done so because of theology alone: it has often been because they have had such hard treatment at the hands of their church or leaders that the whole basis of the faith has been falsified for them. That is tragic, but I rather think God is big enough to somehow hold on to those who have been driven away by the failures of his people. In my case, I set out to follow Jesus, and he led me into deeper understanding, and clearer vision – far from being a slippery slope, he reached down and gave me a leg up to greater heights.

It's been a long journey, and it isn't finished. I often wonder if I'd have been able to travel this way if I wasn't a minister. It's given

me opportunities for study I wouldn't have had, and it's given me
a framework of faith I wouldn't have had: if you're full of doubt
and decide to give church a miss, that's not too big a deal, but if
you're supposed to be leading the service, people notice! Perhaps
God called me because he knew I needed the discipline. I will retire from full-time ministry before very long – but that will enable
me to exercise the ministry to which I feel called, rather than the
ministry to which everyone else thinks I ought to be called. (Well,
that's the plan, and my wife is already making plans for how I'll
be doing it ...) I will still preach and teach, but I will leave the
committees and councils to others, and use music, art and study
to get alongside other people.

From fear to faith. I didn't know it was fear until much later,
but that niggle of cognitive dissonance was fear of being wrong, of
failing to get it right. Well, I'm sure I do get it wrong, but I'm no
longer afraid, because I know I walk with the God who came to us
in Christ. That's faith. And I love it!

7

PENTECOST TO RESURRECTION

The imperfections into which they see themselves fall they bear with humility, meekness of spirit and a loving fear of God, hoping in Him.

REV. MARK STEVENS

INTRODUCTION

The story that follows is personal. It contains details of what I would consider the darkest and yet richest season of my life. I have affectionately dubbed this story "From Pentecost to Resurrection" as a way of describing my journey to faith, into Pentecostalism, and out again. Following two church plants and 10 years within the Pentecostal tradition I found myself on the ministry trash heap. In my mind my faith and career were ruined. My theological world had crumbled. And yet, in spite of it all God made a way through the mess.

I have wanted to be a pastor since I was thirteen. During this dark season of my life I honestly thought it was over. Today it is my honour to pastor the Happy Valley Church of Christ located in Adelaide, South Australia. Once again resurrection power has been at work. Amongst the devastation of breaking away from Pentecostalism and a long journey through the spiritual wilderness I began to rebuild my faith and understanding of the pastoral vocation. At times I barely hung on and yet through it all God was faithful. Resurrection became the defining reality in this wilderness season of my life.

Everyone's journey out of fundamentalism is different. Some, many in fact, hold on to their faith but carry deep pain for most of their life. A pain no one else seems to understand. But I am here to tell you two things I have found to be true. First, God is faithful. Although it may not feel like it, he is. If you are to keep your sanity you must believe this. Second, you will make it. You are stronger than you realise.

I entrust this story to you and I pray that it helps you. Especially pastors who have left churches burnt out and hurt and for pastors who for whatever reasons have had to leave denominations and find themselves lost and wandering in a spiritual wilderness. I will begin by telling you my own journey from Pentecost to Resurrection and then I will employ three metaphors drawn from scripture that have helped me understand the journey I have been on. They are: Easter Saturday, Calling, and Exile.

STORY

When one brings to mind memorable churches the last place anyone would think of is a small chapel in the desert of Arizona. I was 15 and we had been in America for a couple of weeks. As a young boy, my mother and I had travelled around Europe and taken in the wonderful beauty of the Sistine Chapel and visited Westminster Abbey. However, it was a small Catholic church in the middle of the hot Arizona desert that saw the beginnings of my faith and spiritual formation.

From the ages of 5 through until about 8 I attended a local Anglican Church. The people were lovely and used to greet one another with "peace be with you" to which one would respond "and also with you". The Minister, as I remember him, was a very tall man with a warm heart and a cheeky sense of humour. He was the first minister I had ever known and he certainly left me with a positive impression. We attended the church for several years and my experiences within the walls of this beautiful old church gave me a wonderful appreciation of liturgy and tradition. To this day Anglican liturgy feels like home.

During my early teenage years I stopped attending church regularly. However, I could not help but notice a yearning in my heart for a deeper experience of the transcendent. I would often turn to my Children's bible and re-read my favourite Sunday-School stories. When I was young, Sunday School taught me that Jesus was always with me; that he was present to me. I would imagine what it would be like to actually have Jesus with me as a real person – I could introduce him to my friends and play cricket with him! As I grew up I realised that was not going to happen. I was old enough to know that Jesus wasn't real.

And then one day I was standing inside a small Catholic church in the middle of the Arizona desert. As I walked around the small but beautiful underground chapel, I felt an overwhelming sense of the presence of God. It was not an exuberant ecstasy driven experience but rather a sense of peace and closeness with God. All of a sudden my yearnings found what they were looking for. An overwhelming sense of God embraced me. I cannot describe in natural terms what this experience meant to me, except that it changed my life forever. At that moment I knew God was real and that he was with me! To this day I still believe this is the moment I responded to God's salvation call and became a Christian. I simply believed.

Some months after I returned from the United States a friend invited me to go to a youth group run by a local Pentecostal church. After attending the youth group for quite some time, I responded to their "salvation call". The speaker that night told me I was a sinner and I needed to come to Christ, repent of my sin, and ask for forgiveness. It was a guilt driven message in which he had spoken on 'end times.' I was told that if I didn't know Christ, when the trumpet sounded, I would be 'left behind'! That night, inside the home in which we met, even though I didn't feel like a sinner, I responded. If I am honest part of me was scared but for the most part I responded because I wanted to know God more – I felt an irresistible urge to know God personally! And as my hand went up and I prayed the sinner's prayer I was assured that I was now going to heaven if I died. I was fifteen years old.

In my late teens I began attending a mega church of the Pentecostal variety. I quickly became involved in leadership in the youth group and found myself extremely busy. Every night of the week I was doing something at church or for the church. I attended prayer meetings as often as I could and every morning I tried to rise early to pray and read the Bible for this, I was told, is what God wanted from me. It was exciting. The atmosphere of church was electric, charged with a spiritual fervour. It was an energy I had never encountered and it was addictive.

I was 20 when I decided to enroll in a Bible College course. After attending a youth camp in which the speaker had prophesied over me that God had a plan and purpose for my life, I was convinced that God had called me to ministry. For the next three years I was immersed in the Holy Scriptures, stories of the great revivalists, and a mega church culture. Looking back on this time I can say with some gratitude that many good things came out of my time in Bible College. It was not an academically rigorous Bible College but they did love the Bible and they introduced me to study of the Bible and ministry.

It was during my time at Bible College that I began to feel increasingly uncomfortable with the beliefs and practices of the Pentecostal tradition. It isn't that I disagreed with their beliefs because there are many that I still hold to this day. Rather it is the way in which belief was forced upon someone and used as a measuring stick of faith. The culture was equally toxic. Don't get me wrong, for two or more years I craved the power and the passion these people offered me and exuded themselves. I bought front row seats into the culture and zealously pursued ministry in the manner modeled to me. However, as I moved deeper into the culture I began to witness things that would horrify anyone should they be told. I heard pastors speak about people in ways that dehumanized the very souls they called upon to care for. I saw people manipulated in a way I thought would never happen inside a church; oh how naïve I was! And all of it took place behind closed doors. When the lights went down in the sanctuary for the 10am service the bright lights and rock star spectacle blinded what I was seeing. But then it began to happen to me.

Over my final year of Bible College I had begun to question key doctrines and cultural practices. That is when the whispers began. Almost overnight I began to hear things being said about me. I was being avoided and the star which once shone so brightly began to dim. All of a sudden I was no longer a favored child. I was questioning too much. Towards the end of my third year of Bible College I was asked by the then President of the denomination to consider planting a church. Little did I know it at the time but my decision to accept this call would change my life forever. I was bright eyed and bushy tailed. I had finished three years of Bible College and had read Rick Warren's *Purpose Driven Church*. What else was there to know? This was God's call on my life and I was following it with all my zeal. I predicted that the people would turn to Christ in record numbers and that the church would be on the world wide map. But in all honesty, I was doing more leading than following.

I spent 14 months as pastor of that fledgling congregation and when I returned home I did so emotionally and spiritually broken. Where did it all go so wrong I wondered? The precursor to leaving the town and quitting my new church was a hospital stay for stress related issues. I had stressed myself to the point my where my body was reacting. I had tried to live faithfully the call of God upon my life but had done so in my own strength. What was most distressing during this time was that the denomination that called me to plant this church abandoned me as quickly as it sent me. And now I had to recover, alone and afraid. No one was returning my calls. I felt like some kind of spiritual leper; get too close and you'll catch my failure!

This was the beginning of the end. Don't get me wrong: I am to blame as much as anyone for things that would occur down the track. However, I was in my mid-twenties and these people were entrusted with my spiritual care and they failed in that duty of care. These issues still hurt to this day and when people hear me speak of my time at this church there is a still a sense of anger and hurt. As an aside, it has been my experience that such anger and hurt is often dismissed by those who do not understand. Nevertheless, what happened was real and I still carry the scars to prove it.

To cut a very long story short I returned to Adelaide and spent a year out of ministry. It wasn't enough. I accepted a call to help plant another church but this time as an associate Minister. The church quickly grew but the person with whom I was working had emotional problems himself. He was unhealthy to the point of being spiritually abusive. It was during this time that I started an undergraduate degree in ministry. Going to seminary opened up a theological Pandora's Box! Questions I had were opened up for exploration. This began my journey out of Pentecostalism and ministry. If I had thought those years in Bible College and my first church plant were difficult, nothing would compare to what was about to happen. At the end of this time I honestly wondered if I would ever Minister again. I wasn't just burnt out; I was broken.

Let me back the story up a little bit to something that occurred in Bible College. It was the first time I was asked to investigate why I believed what I believed. But it backfired! We were given an assignment relating to our study of the Book of Acts. We had to interview a pastor of another denomination regarding their views concerning baptism of the Holy Spirit and initial evidence. We then had to write a response outlining why they were wrong. I chose a charismatic Baptist minister. It was the first time I had ever heard another argument about baptism in the Holy Spirit from someone who spoke in tongues and yet at the same time believed it was not an initial evidence of baptism in the spirit (if that makes sense). For the first time in Christian walk someone had given voice to questions I was asking. Questions that haunted me for years.

During my early months of my church planting days I sought ordination. As part of that process I was asked to declare my views on the initial evidence of baptism in the spirit. By this time I had settled on my views and they were different to my denomination's views. A fellow pastor knew of my struggles told me to sign the form and then keep quiet. He told me that plenty of guys disagreed and just kept quiet. No one would ever know that I thought differently. I am ashamed to say I signed it. I lied. I was a pastor for 3 years and for three years I wrestled with this issue. I spoke with many colleagues who quietly agreed but told me to shut up for the sake of my career.

Seminary was the first place I had been encouraged to think through theological issues. Instead of telling me what to believe they helped me to evaluate the data and decide for myself while providing a safe place to ask questions and explore my faith. These guys were not liberals either. Many were Pentecostals and Charismatics like me. It was unnerving at first but eventually I relished opportunity to ask questions and "work out my salvation with fear and trembling," as they say. However, with all of this questioning came an increasing unease in my spirit concerning my role within my denomination. I knew in my heart that I could not affirm the central identity marker of the denomination or keep going in the midst of a culture I found I struggled with.

Then the day arrived. I can take you to the exact place where I felt God speak to me (not audibly) and I knew I had to make a decision. Would I continue to keep quiet for the sake of my career or would I show integrity and resign my ordination. I didn't realise it at the time but these issues had been taking a toll far worse than I had realised. I wrote the letter and resigned my position and ministry and my denomination. I didn't mean for it to be a big deal and it wasn't a huge act of protest. Nevertheless, I still felt my career was over. It was to be the beginning of the lowest point of my life when seemingly out of the blue I hit rock bottom.

My wife and I had only been married for a few months when my interior world fell apart. I didn't see it coming. My wife did. Wives are smart like that! One day, not long after I had resigned, we returned home from church and the phone rang. It was our pastor. I can't remember exactly what happened but I will never forget what I felt. My body tensed as though my emotional engine had seized. I would later be told I had burnt out. The burnout related not only to my career but also to my faith. I had been overwhelmed by the years of tension created by the unhealthy system I had been a part of. For years I had bottled things up, I had shut up. And then with the help of some good teachers I had begun to evaluate what I believed. This caused more tension. The bottle eventually exploded under the pressure.

For the next few months I pretty much shut everyone out. I just wanted the world to go away. I would come home from work and shut the blinds and not answer the phone. I lost some friends during this time because they couldn't understand what was going on. From memory I never returned to that church. I needed space and I needed the right kind of support. The pastor continued to hound me and we had to cut our ties. The most disappointing thing through all of this time was the silence and seeming lack of care from the denomination and friends. Very few called and no one really understood. In their mind this all began when I started questioning what they considered the essentials. I was already on the slippery slope. I was left to surmise that no one cared. I was 26 years old. My faith and my dream of being a pastor were over. Little did I know it at the time but I had entered what is described in the book of Jonah as the belly of the whale. Thrown overboard I had been swallowed and now I lay right where God needed me to be.

DEFINING METAPHORS

For some, many perhaps, the journey out of controlling, fundamentalist churches relates to their faith and what they believe. For me this is also true but with the added dimension of losing a career which happened to be closely aligned to my faith. Almost overnight I lost a career, friends and my sense of belonging. I was, in a sense, theologically & vocationally homeless.

It has been 10 years since we left that church and the Pentecostal tradition. It has been a long hard road involving a lot of pain, heart ache and a lot of coming to terms with what happened. Forgiveness has been hard to find but for our own sanity we needed to find it. Moving on has been even harder. But I am pleased to say that after 10 years I am able to look retrospectively at what took place and see how God was at work in the belly of the whale.

As I reflect on what happened I am able to see a conversion taking place. I recently heard author and New Testament scholar Scot McKnight say that all conversion is a form of apostasy. I think he is spot on. What took place had to happen in order for my faith and relationship with God to become what it needed to become. Don't get me wrong, in the midst of it all I was angry, bitter and I wanted revenge. I could never have seen how God was at work. But time has a way of healing wounds and granting wisdom.

What I want to do is provide 3 biblical metaphors that have enabled me to see how God was at work throughout everything that happened. Coming from a prosperity driven culture reflecting and even processing such an experience has been a learning curve. It is my hope these three metaphors will help you in the same way they have helped me.

EASTER SATURDAY

Easter Saturday is the most disorientating of days. The pain and shock of the crucifixion has passed and resurrection is but a dawn away, but we remain in limbo. Not really knowing what to do with ourselves. It is the day of the grave; a day of confusion and reflection. Having walked away from the denomination in which I first heard the call of God to ministry and having all but given up on my faith I now experienced the grave. Death's sting had stung me well. I knew resurrection would come, but when?

Disorientation is the word that best describes the next few years of my life. Leaving a denomination and the safety net of theological belief is akin to divorce. In fact, it is a divorce. It is a tearing apart; a break. I had invested everything I had into them and they had abandoned me. It may sound dramatic but it was a dark time. I needed to leave though; the relationship had become unhealthy.

My wife and I didn't attend church for quite some time. Both of us worked in Christian settings and felt we could sustain our faith apart from the church for a short time. I think it was well over a year before we even visited our first church. It was pushy and demanding. We left it another couple of months before venturing out again. Eventually, after looking at various churches, we found a medium sized congregation that appeared friendly and not too pushy. We never quite fitted in there and didn't really connect with the ethos of the church but it was close and we both felt we needed to re-enter the church culture for the sake of our faith.

It was during this time in the grave that I gave up on ministry all together. The call was gone, dead even. But that is what graves are for, death. For the first time in many years I was forced to consider life apart from ministry. What would I do? Who was I? What would it mean for me to not be a pastor? Luckily (although I didn't realize it at the time) I got a job working as a cleaner (janitor). It was bad for my ego and good for my soul. Every day I emptied rubbish bins and cleaned toilets. But most importantly, I got to know God again. I worked alone and mostly at night which gave me plenty of time to think and pray. I wasn't reading my bible (more on that later) so prayer and reflection sustained my relationship with God. Actually to describe it that way is wrong. Perhaps it would be better to say God sustained me through those times. I cannot recall how many times I would be working and crying thinking about everything that I had gone through and asking God "why?" Silence can be a strange comfort at times.

There are many parts to my Easter Saturday story. It is perhaps the most poignant part of my journey. At times, in fact most of the time, I didn't think I would ever step back into the church let alone ministry. But God is so gracious and loving and even though I doubted, he didn't. It was all a part of the plan. I just wish I had known resurrection was around the corner

THE CALL

The story of Moses comes and goes relatively quickly in Scripture when you consider how long he lived and what he achieved. After he fled the security of Pharaoh's palace Moses had two encounters with Yahweh. In both experiences he came face to face with God. The first, an experience of preparation, began with a burning bush. The second began on Mt Sinai. Both experiences were callings. At the burning bush God called Moses and at Sinai God called Israel. Both times, not without struggle, God called and Moses responded.

I would have been 13 years old when I first heard the call of God to ministry. I was not a Christian (in the traditional sense) and I didn't attend church. Nevertheless, I can take you to the exact spot, the exact place, where I heard the call and knew I wanted to be a minister. There was nothing special about the day and I didn't hear a voice. However, as I rode past a church after school one day I stopped out the front and began to wonder what a life dedicated to God's service would mean. After some time I knew that I wanted to dedicate my life to serving God. I don't know why I thought it, I just did. It was a long road to ordination. From that moment many things began to happen and by the time I was 15 I had received Christ and been baptised (again).

Calling is as unique as the person. How and why God calls us is often beyond our comprehension. What I do know to be true of calling is that it is hard to shake. Looking back on my calling I can say with confidence that I have felt and continue to feel a strong sense of calling. What my belly of the whale experience taught me, what my time as a cleaner taught me, was that before anything else I was called to be a Christian. Then out of my faith flows my vocational calling. My career may have died when I left the Assemblies of God but in rediscovering my call to follow Christ I also discovered my vocational identity. I once again heard the call to be a pastor.

As I mentioned earlier when I left my previous denomination
"I gave up on ministry all together. The call was gone, dead. I was
forced to consider life apart from ministry". I stumbled around like
a blind man groping in the dark for a few years. I was bitter, angry
and, most of all, hurt. It was during this time a friend handed me
Eugene Peterson's *Under the Unpredictable Plant.* They say some
books are chosen and other books choose you. Well Peterson's book
chose me and helped me to once again hear the call. First to Christ
and then to ministry.

In the book Peterson skilfully compares the story of Jonah
with his own personal ministry journey. He calls upon ministers to
remain faithful to the vocation to which they have been called and
not the culture in which they work. Furthermore, he reconnects
the pastoral vocation to our calling to be followers of Jesus. When
I closed the book I turned and picked up my Bible for the first
time in years and discovered what Karl Barth called the strange
new world in the Bible!

EXILE

Exile is the final metaphor I would use to describe leaving a
theological/spiritual tradition. But I would describe it as an exile
from which one may never return (at least in a physical sense).
An exile in which like Israel you learn a lot about yourself, you
move from what Brueggermann calls Orientation, to disorientation
through to reorientation.

Exile is a lonely place. Moving out of something and into
something else is a strange transition. I now minister in a completely different theological tradition (One that I had never heard
of when I was in Bible College). These people speak a completely
different language to me. Their values and beliefs are different to
mine. But they accepted me. They took me in when I needed taking
in and prepared me for ministry.

There is a sense in which I am still pentecostal. But lets call
it a small "p" pentecostal. I still hold to my beliefs about the Holy

Spirit. I still carry my conservative views on Scripture and theology. But I hold these things lightly because they do not define my faith; only Christ can do that. My theology is my way of expressing those things I believe to be true about the Christian life. In Exile I have been able to hold onto those things I have come to appreciate about my past and my Pentecostal heritage.

It is easy to be negative about my time in Pentecostal tradition. However, by God's grace I am learning to see how he has been at work in all of my life. I may be a little embarrassed about the theological shallowness of where I began but truth be told it was a good foundation to build upon and I thank God for it.

For instance, Bible College introduced me to study of the Bible and taught me basic exegesis and the need to set each text in a context. It gave me a passion for the scriptures. Secondly, it introduced me to ministry; not only ministry in a mega church with all the trappings but ministry in smaller rural settings. At least once a month I would travel to small churches to preach. This experience (of preaching) and witnessing what actually goes into pastoring a small church was a real blessing. Thirdly, the Pentecostals gave me an appreciation of the work of the Holy Spirit and how it related to ministry practice. God was alive and Scripture was believed to be a living and breathing Word from God. In many ways they gave me spirituality adequate for this time of exile!

Taking Responsibility

The biggest growth area in my life over the past year or two has been an acceptance of my past story as a good and even positive part of my life. It can be incredibly difficult to acknowledge pain and disappointment as a positive part of who I am in Christ however, I think this is what God would want for me. It has been a big part of healing and moving on.

I was, for 12 or so years, a Pentecostal. The Pentecostal tradition baptised me into the Christian faith and then trained me for ministry. And then as you have just read it went pear shaped. I was angry, really angry. For years I would snidely remark to anyone who would listen that before I was a Christian I was a Pentecostal. What a terrible thing to say. But I said it out of hurt and shame. Don't get me wrong, there is a lot about modern Pentecostalism that concerns me but much of it isn't theological, it is practical. But staying bitter and angry is akin to drinking poison and expecting your enemy to die!

I am not sure when it all began to change for me but some time ago I began to write down my story. I called it, From Pentecost to Resurrection. What you have just read is the finished product. It detailed how I became a Christian and how I soon became caught up in the world of Pentecostalism and mega-church ministry. I drank the kool-aid and I drank it good. The first few drafts of the story were negative and critical. Over time I began to edit them. In this process something in me began to change. God began to bring about emotional healing. It culminated when I took personal responsibly for what happened, when I owned up to the fact that what happened to me at the hands of people charged with the care of my soul was partly my fault, God began to work. I accepted responsibility. From that point on I began to see and appreciate the many good things that God did in me during this season of my life and forgiveness towards those who hurt me began to be extended. Now don't get me wrong, it is an ongoing struggle and I can never see myself returning to the Pentecostal tradition. But for me at least resurrection has come. The tomb is empty. Why would I stay there? I have a whole life ahead of me.

If I am honest, my time within Pentecostalism did more to teach me how to be a good pastor than any course I have taken. Each one of us who have transitioned out of fear can move towards a free and genuine faith. Each one of us, I am convinced, can experience the wonderful power of resurrection. Of course for me the tale is called "From Pentecost to Resurrection" but the first word will be different for each person.

As I mentioned earlier, paramount to making it through this experience was finding spirituality. For a long time I thought it was about theology, and don't get me wrong theology is important, but far more important was an adequate spirituality grounded in prayer and God's word. Also, a robust education was incredibly helpful for helping me explore the boundaries of my own faith. For a long time I thought I was heading down a slippery slope when in fact quite the opposite was true. Instead of heading away from orthodoxy I was moving toward it for myself. What I once believed I pretty much still believe but now Jesus is at the centre.

8

SOCIAL CONSTRUCTION, FUNDAMENTALISM, & THE READING OF SCRIPTURE

OR –

HOW STUDYING SOCIOLOGY SAVED MY THEOLOGY

DANIEL ORTIZ

It was April 2003, I was married with one daughter, when I heard that I was accepted into the University of Sheffield's Master course in Sociological Research. I applied to this course partly because I find social sciences fascinating and partly looking to change academic careers. You see, before that, in 2001 I graduated with a Masters in Theology from the Queen's University of Belfast (QUB). Most of the previous decade was spent in theological studies at two different academic institutions, both of them Christian, both of them Evangelical.

After graduation I experienced the same frustrating realization that theological students feel when they finish their studies, I found no suitable employment. Unless a theological student is going through to full time Christian work, or into academic work, the jobs are simply not there. The feeling is magnified the higher the academic degree you have, trust me. As life takes over, I was forced to find work even outside of my training. So I decided to re-train, but, being the book reading type, I decided to retrain academically and not practically.

What I didn't know was that the following two years would be of intellectual and spiritual development for me. As I began to understand sociological theory and research methods better, I began to view the world differently. I began to view my faith differently. By the time my studies had finished, I had deconstructed and re-constructed my faith. Many of the beliefs and doubts I held before were challenged. I was able to view my faith afresh through the eyes of social science. One of my favorite sociological quotes is from C Wright Mills, he says:

> "It is the political task of the social scientist ... continually to translate personal troubles into public issues, and public issues into the terms of their human meaning."

I like this quote because it maps out the change I went through. I learnt to verbalize my personal beliefs as social constructs, and those constructs into human meaning. In deed my faith was saved by sociology. It truly reminds me of Peter's admonition "Always be prepared to give an answer to everyone who asks you to give the reason for the hope that you have" (1 Peter 3:15). But how did sociology save my theology? and how does that affect how we read Scripture? Let me show you.

FUNDAMENTALISM?

I will like to discuss what is meant by "Fundamentalism." As with all religious terminology, fundamentalism is not easily pinned down to a singular definition. It is subjective and descriptive in normal day use, and it fails to actually portray what is meant by "fundamentalism."

It is no secret that the term "Fundamental", when speaking within a Christian background, has its origins in the documents written between 1910-1915 known as "The Fundamentals". This set of 12 volumes was written as means to preserve and promote a reformed, conservative and, in my opinion, uniquely American set of theological beliefs. The basics of the basics with which all protestant Christians could agree. Of course Inerrancy was major point, but also was the person of Jesus, the inequality of modern sciences and philosophies, the true Church and Salvation by faith alone, amongst others. These are commonly known to be the source of Christian fundamentalism, making fundamentalism at the most, just over a century old phenomenon.

However, I'm not entirely convinced that fundamentalism as we know it originated with these. In the case of B. B. Warfield, we have one of the main authors, (wrote on the divinity of Jesus), who is willing to contemplate Darwinian evolution and does not find it in opposition to Christian theology. By the modern standards of fundamentalists, he would be considered a liberal. The Fundamentals might have started the movement, but it is the development that really counts.

James Barr, Scottish theologian and biblical scholar, recognized in his book Fundamentalism, that there are two expressions of fundamentalism. One is a militant, separatist and anti-intellectual social movement; and the other is a theological mentality whose identity is invested in an "inerrant" Bible that creates a set of special hermeneutics in order to maintain plausibility. Sociologist Jeffrey Hadden arrives to a similar conclusion regarding fundamentalism as a social movement. He observes that the Scopes trial of the 1920's is the true beginning of fundamentalism as an anti-scientific and separatist political movement. He also observes that, as a term, fundamentalism was solely used in reference to American Christian Fundamentalism before the Iranian revolution of 1979, when the media conveyed the term Islamic Fundamentalism.

Bergler, in his book *The Juvenalization of American Christianity* gives a feasible account of how the social conditions in the United States, and not just conservative theology, gave rise to the theological form of Christian fundamentalism. He argues that:

> Beginning in the 1930s and 1940s, Christian teenagers and youth leaders staged a quiet revolution in American church life which can properly be called the juvenalization of Amer-

ican Christianity. Juvenalization is the process by which the religious beliefs, practices, and ... characteristics of adolescents become accepted as appropriate for Christians of all ages... with both youth and adults embracing immature versions of the faith.[1]

This quiet revolution, Bergler continues, didn't happen in a vacuum, but instead, was the result of an underlying fear found in their parents. Fear that, after WWII, America was going to be swept away by a crisis of civilization, that there would be an end to "economic prosperity, democracy, and religious freedom." Bergler concludes that it is this juvenile form of Christianity that we find now rampant in the United States.

So we have fundamentalism, which is a separatist, anti-intellectual, political movement, and fundamentalism which is a theological perspective. In addition to this I would add that Christian fundamentalism is intrinsically an American phenomenon, or at least American in origin. It was the American culture wars of the 20th Century that developed fundamentalism into what we see now. Both expressions of fundamentalism find significant overlaps with American nationalism, more so than in any other country. I am saying this not as a critic of American Christians, but, in the spirit of James Barr, I'm identifying why it would be so difficult for American Christians to differentiate between the nationalism, political ideology and theological perspective, especially since it has now been morphed to mean any sort of religious, conservative, and, politically right-wing drive or perspective. When we compare the likes of Liberation Theology, for example, although being a religious-driven social theology, it is not assumed to be fundamentalist because it is politically socialist.

In my experience, fundamentalism in Bolivia, where I am from, was more of a theological perspective instead of a social one.

---

1 http://www.huntington.edu/News-Releases/Academics/Ministry-and-Missions/The-Juvenilization-of--American-Christianity/ (last accessed 5/5/2013).

Most of the social aspect of fundamentalism had no relevance to Protestant/Evangelicals because the Roman Catholic Church, the national church, already covered most of them, even though the Roman Church was/is regarded as the Great Babylon of the Book of Revelation. I don't believe that I was raised in a fundamentalist household, partly due to my parent's academic training and partly because Bolivia is 90% Roman Catholic. However, in hindsight, I can clearly see how the special fundamentalist hermeneutics were introduced and fostered even in theological training. If there is anything positive to be said of fundamentalist Christians, it is the way they propagate their beliefs in books, radio and TV. This might seem as if I am praising their "globalization mentality". In fact, I am criticizing non-fundamentalist theologians and scholars for not keeping up with their efforts. For example, Wayne Grudem's *Systematic Theology* has been translated into Spanish and is easily available throughout Hispanic America. Answers in Genesis have produced Ken Ham's DVDs in over 100 different languages. If the purpose of scholarship is to educate, Western scholarship has failed where fundamentalists have triumphed.

This special hermeneutics I am referring to is a way to view the "Bible", especially the Protestant Bible. The theological doctrines of Inerrancy, Infallibility, and Sola Scriptura are amalgamated into one, with no discussion of similarities, differences of relevance. In some cases they are not even known as such. They are overridden by the more recent "Literalism" type of hermeneutics. This means that, the Bible can only be taken literally as the Bible is a type of Divine receiver on earth. The writers of the Bible were themselves simple pens who may not have even known what they were writing. And it also assumes that the modern reader will receive "divine revelation" at the moment of reading. In fact, the closest comparison that I can come up with is that this special hermeneutic makes the Bible little more than the Prophecies of Nostradamus.

These special hermeneutics don't apply only to what is written in the Bible, it applies to everything that surrounds it. From the number of books it has, the correct translation, to the doctrines of

Sola Scriptura, inerrancy and infallibility. This special hermeneutics or special perspective on the Bible creates an alternative universe where the Bible is uniquely positioned as intercessory between God and man.

It is this hermeneutic that I moved away from, in a slow process that is intimately linked to my own academic training at QUB, Northern Ireland. For my dissertation, I decided to study the relationship between the Catholic Church and the Protestant Church. However, being a foreigner, I wouldn't have dared to apply it to the Northern Irish "troubles". Not even for a PhD!!! Instead I decided to focus on the aforementioned relationship in the context of Bolivia. The Reformation and Counter-reformation were major areas of my research, and this is where I had some serious realizations, none other than with the doctrine of Sola Scriptura.

Sola Scriptura alone would fill a ridiculous number of books so I will not cover it in-depth but simply introduce it for context. Alongside Sola Fide (Faith Alone), Sola Gratia (Grace Alone), Solo Christo (Christ Alone), and Soli Deo Gloria (Glory to God Alone), they form the core (or fundamental) doctrines from the Reformers. Sola Scriptura, in particular, was the defining doctrine of the Reformation. It states that Scripture Alone is the inspired and authoritative revelation from God. That besides it there is no need for human authority on matters of faith and doctrine. This placed Scripture in direct opposition to the Papacy at the time of the Reformation as primary source of authority.

It was during this research that I was introduced to the work of H. Richard Niebuhr and his social theory approach to theology. In his *The Social Sources of Denominationalism*, Niebuhr made it very clear that theological differences are not theological in origin, but social instead. For a young theologian that had been taught to believe, and defend to some degree, the most basic tenets of the protestant faith (the Fundamentals if you will), it was fascinating to find another, significantly plausible explanation that challenged those beliefs.

I took my cue from Niebuhr and noticed some interesting sociological happenings. For example, infallibility, a key doctrine behind Sola Scriptura, was not Protestant in origin. In fact, this was a doctrine already in use to describe Papal authority, ex cathedra of course. I noticed that:

The Protestant doctrine of Infallibility of Scripture was developed after the development of the doctrine of the Infallibility of the Pope. The first developed as a counter measure to outweigh the latter.

I concluded that the doctrine of Sola Scriptura grew out of the social and political movements of the reformation, that it was less theology and more policy. Some may agree with my assessment or not, but, we cannot avoid realizing that people, not just revelation, were the sources of theology. Back then I couldn't articulate it, but in hindsight I was referring to social construction.

SOCIAL CONSTRUCTION

As with Sola Scriptura, social construction, also known as social learning or social knowledge, could fill many books in order to explain it thoroughly. Instead, I will briefly present the theory and its relevance to this topic. If you would like to familiarize yourself more with the theory, may I suggest Berger's and Luckmann's *The Social Construction of Reality*.

Social Construction is basically the recognition that the human world is humanly constructed, nothing new there. To say it differently, things could not have existed if society had not built them; and if society had been different, they would have been built differently or not at all. Everything from the human world is constructed, which means, by contrast, nature is not. Nature, thus, is referred to "real" as opposed to "construct." However, it is not just things that are constructed; the mechanisms of our world are also constructed. The ideas, ideologies, culture, perspectives, the way we learn, the way we think, these are all constructs. We built reality around us.

The implication of this theory to religion is paramount. In his book *The Sacred Canopy*, Berger explores the social construction of religion. He concludes that religion is born out of the society it comes from, forming a sacred canopy over their world in order to give it meaning, hence the title. Taking this theory to its fullest meaning for religion we can safely argue that religion is a social construct, theology is a social construct, the church, the doctrines of Sola scriptura, the Bible, and even the concept of God are all socially constructed.

At this point some people would assume that this is a death blow for my personal beliefs. Nothing could be further from the truth. It is through a detailed understanding of the theory and not a simplistic view of it that we can see theological significance in it. The fact that some things are constructs does not mean they are fictional or made up. The classic example of the car, when asking, "is it real or constructed?" we might be tempted to answer "constructed." The real answer is "depends at the speed is going". You see, if a car is doing 30 mph towards you, it becomes a real (natural) danger. If the car is doing 0 mph, the car is a unnatural human construction of metal, rubber, plastic, etc. Social construction and nature are not mutually exclusive; more often than not, they complement each other.

Another example is the natural sciences. They are constructed, but what science teaches us about nature is not made up. A final example, the quark: is it real (natural)? Or constructed? Some people would say that it is natural because it is something we found in nature. However, how did we find it? Was it using our senses or did we construct the means and the theory that allowed us to find it? The quarks in this case is both, real and constructed, because the quark is found in nature; we didn't create it. But the concept of the quark is constructed, because we created the means to find it. This is the real beauty of social constructionism, because it explains how we know without explaining it away.

When we apply social construction to reading the Bible, we can see the layers of human involvement in it. I will summarize them but bear in mind that I am not a biblical scholar so I might miss some. Starting from a simple reading of the Bible itself:

» We know that they were originally written in Hebrew, Greek and Arameic, so it is vitally important that we understand these.

» But language itself is a construct, so each word can carry many meanings, so these meaning must be understood also.

» Meaning is dependent on the cultural background, so we must also understand the culture behind the meaning.

» Culture in itself is an amalgamation of the history, the experiences, the technology, and the economy of the people. We must understand these, but also understand that they change with time.

» There was a point where the authors no longer had control over their writings and the scribes, compilers/editors copied and/or decided which books were to be included. Their culture and language must be understood as well.

» Now we have the primitive translators and commentators. How about their language, their culture, their ideologies?

» With the protestant Bible we now must include the Reformers' input into which books should be included, and how any specific passages should be interpreted.

» In addition, we must include the translations being read. Even the most correct translation to the originals was translated by consensus in a community effort.

» And lastly is the Bible version being read of any specific denominational background? The denomination's history and theology must also be known.

» This is just half the story; this is the Bible's side. The readership also has layers:

» What age is he/she?

» What level of education does he/she have?

» Is he/she reading in his/hers native language? Or reading in a different language?

» Has he/she been trained to read Biblical Hebrew, Koine Greek, Aramaic, (Latin I'm told is useful).

» Is he/she trained in archeology?

» Can he/she read English, German and French? (most often used languages in biblical scholarship.)

» Has he/she been trained in cross cultural analysis?

» Is he/she politically conservative? politically liberal?

» Is he/she in poverty or wealthy?

» Is he/she in love? (I'm told it affects the brain cells.)

All these layers added to the layers in the bible make up one enormous undertaking that flies in the face of a simple, literal reading of Scripture. It is clear to me that Scripture was written and passed down to us by a huge communal enterprise. When we 'read' Scripture, we are not only reading a book, we are reading the community that produced it. We must recognize that when we 'read' Scripture we are being part of and continuing this communal enterprise. And, from a theological perspective, this is the way that was intended by God, as Jesus said in Matthew 18:18-20:

> I tell you the truth, whatever you bind on earth will be bound in heaven, and whatever you loose on earth will be loosed in heaven. Again, I tell you that if two of you on earth agree about anything you ask for, it will be done for you by my Father in heaven. For where two or three come together in my name, there am I with them.

In fact, the special hermeneutics that demand we read the text in a specific way (literalistic), are a relatively new development, which the authors of Scripture never intended to be read like. The special hermeneutics are thus a corruption of the original perspective on Scripture. Inerrancy specifically, is a classic example of what Weber calls the mutual interaction between ideas and behaviour: ideas shape behaviour, and behaviour shapes ideas. At the end we are left with an idea (inerrancy) that does not match its original form. I would have to say that a simplistic reading of scripture is impossible. Even in the best case scenario of a trained Biblicist, who is an expert in ancient languages, knows the archaeology behind the text, has spent decades in academia, and was able to travel back in time to witness the events first hand, it's highly improbable.

READING SCRIPTURE

I finished my sociological studies having several epiphanies along the way. I came out with a greater understanding on how my faith had been constructed and passed down to me. I was able to verbalize more intelligently how and why I believed. As I said before, sociology saved my theology.

Regarding scripture, I realized a number of facts that I find useful to keep in mind when reading it. These are my realizations, so they work for me, they might not work for you or might do, but here they are anyway:

I realized that the Bible is not one book, but a bookshelf of books. This may sound obvious but how many times do we confuse the meaning of one book with another. Each book was written independently (to a certain degree) and should have no bearing over the meaning of the other. Just because Genesis is considered mythology (actually mythology and folklore to be precise) it does not have any bearing on the historicity of Jesus.

I realized that the Old Testament was written from the viewpoint of the Hebrews, the New Testament was written from a perspective of the early church. We can't expect them to say any-more than that. This does not mean they cannot speak to us today, but they are not written for us.

I realized that Scriptures were passed down to us through a huge social undertaking. We must accept that as individuals we can't make sense of it without the help of others, guides, commen-taries, etc.

I realized that there is a culture surrounding how we read Scripture. This culture can change or remain but it is not intrinsic to the actual text nor to our relationship with God.

I realized that the Scriptures demand a level of commitment in their study. A single reading will always be simplistic, so diligence is a requisite.

I realized that Scriptures are not God to be worshiped, but are still inspired by God. (I'm still working on this one.)

I realized that not all will read the same passage and agree with me, and that is fine.

Nothing that I've said is really new. You could read Catholic, Protestant, and Orthodox theology and will find the same or similar views there. The only difference is that the original doctrines have been sadly developed into the special hermeneutics I've discussed above. My realizations are simply a call to re-examine assumptions and revisit the basics.

One final word on fundamentalists and leaving fundamen-talism. Not all fundamentalists are intrinsic fundamentalists; they might only have fundamentalist leanings, something they've picked up along the way mostly because of the century they were born in. The way they are treated by those that leave fundamentalism will either strengthen those leanings or loosen them.

If you are in the process of leaving fundamentalism, make sure you know what type of fundamentalism you are leaving. It is very easy to think that one is the other, or by leaving a type of funda-mentalism you are leaving all types. It is possible to stop being a fundamentalist and still remain active in conservative politics and remain conservative on moral issues. It is also possible to leave fundamentalism and still be a committed Evangelical. What is not possible is to leave fundamentalism without a renewing of the mind. St Paul tells us this even back at the beginning: "to put off your old self, which belongs to your former manner of life and is corrupt through deceitful desires, and to be renewed in the spirit of your minds." For this renewal to happen, a correct attitude towards reading Scripture is essential.

9

GROWING UP AT THE END OF THE WORLD

*It befits the soul, however, to contrive to labour, in so far as it can, on its
own account, to the end that it may purge and perfect itself, and thus may
merit being taken by God into that Divine care wherein it becomes healed
of all things that it was unable of itself to cure.*

CAITLIN G. TOWNSEND

*Whosoever shall not receive the kingdom of God as a little child,
he shall not enter therein.*   (Mark 10:15)

It was the middle of a warm May night when I was roused
by hands shaking me gently and then picking me up. I sleepily
clutched a stuffed cat as my father loaded me into the front pas-
senger seat of our Chevy sedan without shoes on. I contemplated
how strange it felt not to be wearing shoes in the car. And then we
were following the ambulance.

My mother would later tell me that she'd died on that ambulance, but God had sent her back to take care of my father and me.
I wasn't sure why she wasn't in the car with us, nor was I particularly
aware of the reason those blue lights were flashing ahead of the
windshield. We softly glided through the countryside, ghostly and
diffuse in the moonlight. I wasn't afraid, exactly – I didn't know
what to fear. I watched the trees go by, numb.

After an interminable night in a gray-tinged, boxlike waiting
room, I was ushered into a sterile white room to hold my mother's
hand. She smiled weakly, not yet able to explain what had happened. I was just glad to know she was still there. Later I learned
that my mother had gone to the hospital expecting my younger

brother and come home without him. With the end of her pregnancy came the end of the life we thought we had.

The trauma sent my mother into the arms of her homeschooling friend, and from there to the crushing embrace of her friend's fundamentalist church. Borrowing from the fundamental Baptist and Pentecostal traditions, our new church embraced Creationism, the culture wars, traditional gender roles, quiverfull family planning, and fire and brimstone preaching. A host of changes awaited me as my mother learned to seek the Holy Spirit. First to go were swimsuits and pants, then bangs, then makeup, then music and movies, then Christmas. In their place came Wednesday night Bible studies, Beautiful Girlhood books, long prairie skirts and Elsie Dinsmore. But beneath these superficial changes lay another, deeper shift. When I was six, the world lay in front of me, ready to be seized and crafted into whatever my heart desired. When I turned seven, I realized that I was growing up at the end of the world.

"You should talk to Jesus like he's your best friend, sitting right next to you."

Talking to Jesus seemed to require a lot of instruction. My pastor told stories of hearing God's voice in his mind, calling him to ministry. My mother had long conversations with God between the Bible and her diary. Theirs was a written love affair. When I opened my Bible at random, trying on her strategy, I found only nonsensical fragments of history, proverbs and lists of names. I knew that nothing else in my life mattered as much as learning to talk to Jesus – and to listen to him as he talked to me. But I couldn't shake the feeling that he must not like me very much. After all, nobody else had left so many messages on his voice mail. If they had, they weren't telling.

More tangible relationships weren't much simpler. I found myself at sea in the crowd of little girls at my church. Our lives looked nothing like one another. They had siblings by the dozen, and I was an only child. They talked of future husbands and wedding songs and raising their little siblings. I wanted to climb trees and dress up like a lion. So I sought refuge amongst the boys, who could more easily be persuaded to pull off a masked train robbery on their parents' sofa cushions. I had no idea that this was controversial.

I was not yet eight when I was first accused of being a temptation to the boys in my church. I didn't know yet that it was because friendships between the sexes were frowned upon – I just thought something was wrong with me. This problem, however, would only grow as I did. The more I stretched and reached up toward the world of adults, the less I recognized or wanted what I found. Like Alice in Wonderland, I found my limbs outgrowing the house I was meant to occupy.

By the time I was fourteen, I had come to the realization that there was only one way to be a woman of God, and that I would never attain it. Not that I couldn't – physically, I was pretty sure that I could. What I needed to do was get married, bear children, and submit my will to my husband's for life. It sounded simple enough. The cost though, was my soul, my life, and my conscience.

Two babies were born, shrieking, in the curtained white rooms of a New Jersey hospital. It was the 1980s, and we were swaddled in soft terry blankets by nurses with enormous hair. One was a boy. He would grow up to hear that the world was his oyster – true or not, he at least believed that he had a choice about what kind of life to live. But the other child was a girl, and all you needed to know about her future lay between her legs. And from the bottom of my heart, I knew that this was wrong.

I believed that the Word of God was infallible and perfect. I believed that Jesus was God and that he'd died for my sins. I believed that he was coming back soon to catch away his Bride in a glorious rapture of the elect. But I could not – did not, ever – believe that women were born to obey men. No amount of prayer, or tears, or repentance, or Bible studies, or rousing sermons, or terror of death, could uproot the conviction that gender inequality was not justice. It could not be the creation of a just God.

"His ways are higher than our ways," I was told.

Then I'd stick to the low road and take my chances.

My only solace was nature. Walking in the green, watching the wildlife, holding my beloved pet cats – these things reminded me that there was love in the world. Not the aching, dying love of the cross. That was not the kind of love I needed to sustain me. What I needed was the peace in the summer breeze, the miracle of the first crocus of the spring, the softness of the bright white snow, the gentle caution of the deer grazing outside my window, the contented purr of the kitten in my arms. It was this perfect love, the energy that sustained the universe, that breathed life back into my battered soul, that I clung to with a desperate, final grip. If the whole world burned, I would burn with it.

The church split my family like a stroke of lightning, cauterizing the seams and ensuring that nothing would ever fit together smoothly again. No glue could repair a burn. My parents' marriage dissolved in a cloud of rage and tears. Our extended family looked on, confused, unsure how a church could ever insert itself so firmly in a family that it could not extricate itself without breaking apart.

When I was fourteen, I began to feel the hatred of the God of my church in full force. My pastor preached from a sermon by faith healing minister William Branham that God had turned over the design of the female body to Satan at the Creation. Women, he said, were created to tempt men into sin. Whenever a man looked at a woman lustfully, he continued, that woman was responsible for adultery with that man. At the Last Judgment, she would answer for infidelity and for sending his soul to hell.

The hits kept coming. Women were weaker vessels, the sermons ran, and more easily tempted. That's why God had ordained that each woman have a male "head," whom she must obey and honor as her "lord." As the daughter of a single mother, I secretly relished my headlessness and resolved to keep it that way.

"Paul said it's better to be single," I hedged, when older women in the church opined about my marriage prospects. Other times, I openly said, "I don't think I'm being called to be a wife and mother."

All women, I was taught, had an innate maternal instinct and the desire to be protected. I searched myself, came up dry, and decided that I must have a male soul and be stuck in the wrong body.

My body kept getting in my way. I wrapped my budding chest in constricting fitness clothes. I draped myself in thick, baggy fabrics. All this concealment just kept failing – I would still catch a man leering outside the gas station, I would still elicit some comment from my father about my "womanly" figure. Shame saturated my mind. What had I done wrong, that God had made me a woman?

I stopped eating.

I dropped a third of my body weight in the desperate attempt to hide the tempting curves that made me a child adulteress whenever I walked to the post office or the corner store. I immersed myself in the Bible, throwing away and deleting and burying all the distracting pleasures I'd let into my life. Days I spent in studious prayer, chewing doggedly on rinsed gum to stave off hunger. Nights, I cried for hours to be filled with the Holy Spirit – to have wicked desires for independence, for a job, for a life outside the home, be taken from me if God truly wanted me to be somebody I wasn't.

Sometimes I dreamed that there were many Gods – one for every planet, every life form. I had just been unlucky to be born in this one's kingdom. Maybe there was a God somewhere who ruled with love and justice, who didn't create inferior beings with the capacity to know that they were inferior. I imagined that somewhere, there was a world without hell, without hierarchy, without the pain of betrayal by one's own body. I wondered if that God and ours had an ancient rivalry.

I knew they were heresies, but I was too tired to care. I was pretty sure that I was a vessel of dishonor, anyway, and the end was coming tomorrow.

Some animal instinct forced me to eat again, even when fueling my temptress body was the last thing I wanted to do. The sight of my bones had given me some comfort. Their rigid, angular projections protected me from the soft, dangerous curves of womanhood. But there were signs of another escape on the horizon: I turned 18, and I got a job.

I realized that as long as I remained pure, nobody could find fault with my working. I grew deaf to the judgments of the older women in my church, admonishing me to keep at home. I began to listen, instead, to the hopeful voice of my mother, who had worked her way through school in the 1970s and wanted me to have the same chance she did.

It was at school, in a night classroom taught by a brilliant and eccentric man with a passion for Madonna and Walt Whitman, that I came alive. One evening, as I packed up my books, the professor stopped me to ask if I'd ever thought about writing for a living. I caught my breath, whirling to stare at him as if he'd held out a million dollars. *You can do it*, the professor promised. *You're smart.*

The borders of my world seemed to explode, running out in all directions like shock waves from an earthquake. *I could escape?* I felt like I'd just been told that I could go to the moon. I recalled a billboard I'd seen the previous year: "From Homeless to Harvard," the story of a poor girl at community college who turned her life into something unrecognizably wonderful. I could be that girl who overcame, who rejected the life laid out before her and forged a new one. I could make something of myself. *I could be that girl.*

When I graduated with my master's degree a few years ago, I found myself standing at a bus stop and wondering what I would say if I met my teenage self. That sad girl, engulfed in denim waves and bruised with the attacks of Bible verses wielded to keep her in the house, to keep her afraid and in chains. Would she be afraid of this new me? The person she was terrified to dream of becoming? What could I possibly tell her?

I would ask her to take a walk in the woods with me. I would show her the cautious deer, the busy squirrels, the steady growth of the pale green saplings, the sturdiness of the ancient trees. I would ask her to listen to the purring of a cat, to hold out her hand for a puppy to lick.

She didn't need to prepare to leave the world. She didn't need to believe in a God who made her his enemy. She didn't need to try to cut off parts of her soul to fit a narrow mould. She didn't need to sing, "This world is not my home." She didn't need to worry about what kind of God would create a kingdom of the fearful and the obedient, would take a Bride from those who left millions behind to die.

This is the kingdom of God.

I believed a lot of things as a child, because I had to. My list is much shorter now. I believe in love and justice, in equality. I believe that nature brings us closer to the spirit of God than any words ever could. And while I no longer flip through the pages of the Bible, seeking instructions, I know in my bones that the closest I've ever come to being led by God was when I gradually, gingerly, stepped away from fundamentalism, following the truth in my heart.

10

DIVINE DISENCHANTMENT: TRANSITIONS & ASSISTING THOSE IN RELIGIOUS MIGRATION

JOHN W. MOREHEAD[1]

ABSTRACT

Reliable statistical data from social science research indicates that thousands of Latter-day Saints leave the Mormon Church each year. Over time, these individuals adopt a variety of irreligious and religious pathways in reaction to their prior Mormon experience. Although much focus has been given to the study of religious affiliation, very little attention has been given to the processes of religious disaffiliation and reaffiliation (religious switching), and

1 2012 Salt Lake Sunstone Symposium and Workshops presentation, July 29, 2012. John W. Morehead (MA, Salt Lake Theological Seminary) is the Custodian of the Western Institute for Intercultural Studies, and the Director of the Evangelical Chapter of the Foundation for Religious Diplomacy. His academic focus is in the areas of new religious movements (with special interest in Mormonism and Paganism), interreligious dialogue, and religion and popular culture. He is the co-editor and contributing author for *Encountering New Religious Movements: A Holistic Evangelical Approach* (Kregel Academic, 2004), the editor of *Beyond the Burning Times: A Pagan and Christian in Dialogue* (Lion, 2008), and editor of *Sacred Tribes Journal*.

how this journey relates to new destinations for former Mormons. Multidisciplinary material exists that can serve in the creation of resources to those making a spiritual migration from one religious group to another. In order to address this deficit, this essay will discuss the background behind *Transitions*, a new video and workbook resource designed for immigrants shifting from Mormonism to more traditional forms of Christianity. It will consider the reality of religious disaffiliation and switching; the perspective and needs of the former LDS transitioner; the multidisciplinary perspectives, resources, and strategy that inform *Transitions*; and how religious institutions might better assist those making the journey from one religious tradition to another.

INTRODUCTION

Protestant evangelical Christianity and Mormonism are missionary religions. That is, the adherents of these religious groups believe in the unique truth claims of their religions, and they believe that they have a responsibility to share their religion while inviting others to be a part of its ranks. This missionary mandate also includes viewing representatives of each other's religious traditions as potential members, and as a result, there is a missionary flow between each religious tradition to the other. This has resulted in a tension between the two groups, with accusations of sheep stealing. As sensitive as this topic might be, the point to keep in mind for the purposes of this present discussion is that migration happens in both directions between the two groups.

In addition to this dynamic, statistical data indicates that a large number of Latter-day Saints choose to leave Mormonism, and move to other metaphysical locations. This includes the skeptical destinations of atheism and agnosticism, as well as various new religious communities, including the New Spirituality and various aspects of Western esotericism, as well as the synthesis of aspects of

Mormonism with other pathways.[2] In addition, a sizeable number retain an interest in Jesus and Christianity, but seek ways in which to express this without the connections to the LDS Church.

Religious switching happens. It is a fact of our pluralistic times in which religious options are as plentiful as the options for beverages or automobiles. But making the migration from Mormonism to more traditional forms of Christianity is far more stressful and challenging than shifting one's preference from Dr. Pepper to 7Up, or from Ford to Toyota. Religious immigrants face a host of challenges and are in need of resources to assist them in their journey. This seminar will discuss the planning and strategy behind *Transitions*, a new multimedia resource designed to assist those who have made the decision to leave Mormonism and migrate into traditional forms of Christianity. *Transitions* was conceived of and co-executive produced by Ken Mulholland, President of the Western Institute for Intercultural Studies,[3] and myself as the Director of WIIS.

In considering the process of religious disaffiliation and reaffiliation, rather than emphasizing the destination, this paper will focus on issues related to the journey itself, and how religious institutions can be more sympathetic and helpful to those making the journey of immigration, whatever direction that migration might be taking the individual.[4]

---

2 For an exploration of this phenomenon see Doe Daughtrey's PhD dissertation through Arizona State University on the synthesis of Mormonism with the New Spirituality and Neopaganism.

3 WIIS is a non-profit religious organization that specializes in research and education for evangelicals related to new religious movements and world religions found at http://www.wiics.org.

4 Although this paper touches on issues related to worldview transformation, it does not emphasize this aspect, or in presenting a winsome presentation of the evangelical understanding of the traditional Christian story. On the process of worldview transformation from the perspective of missiology see Paul G. Hiebert, *Transforming Worldviews: An Anthropological Understanding of How People Change* (Grand Rapids: Baker Academic, 2008).

RELIGIOUS SHOPPING AND DISAFFILIATION

In the past, cultures provided little diversity by way of options for religious belief. One's religious life was largely determined by place of birth. Although this still plays a large part in individual religious convictions, we now live in a global village with media connectivity attached to consumerism that provides for a host of options, not only for consumers of goods and services, but also for religion and spirituality. This means that not only are we learning more about religious options in the marketplace, but also that exchanges between individuals of differing religious traditions, including evangelistic interactions, are taking place. Often times the result of this shopping from America's religious smorgasbord is switching from one religious group to another. Survey data confirms that this process is taking place.

In 2008 the Pew Forum released its U.S. Religious Landscape Survey, and followed this up in 2009 with a report titled "Faith in Flux: Changes in Religious Affiliation in the U.S.[5] This report was somewhat surprising in that it revealed a greater fluidity in religious affiliation than had previously been recognized.[6] In the 2007 survey 28% of American adults had changed religious affiliation, but the data from the 2009 report "suggest that previous estimates actually may have understated the amount of religious change taking place in the U.S."[7] Respondents indicated that they left their previous religion for a variety of reasons, but disenchantment with religious institutions and religious people were significant reasons cited.

Many traditional religious institutions are struggling in the present late modern or postmodern and post-Christendom envi-

---

5 Online document available at http://www.pewforum.org/Faith-in-Flux.aspx.

6 Consider the claim of Rodney Stark and Roger Finke that "fewer than 1 percent of Americans convert." Rodney Stark and Roger Finke, *Acts of Faith: Explaining the Human Side of Religion* (University of California Press, 2000), 115.

7 "Faith in Flux," Executive Summary, 3.

ronment, and this includes the Church of Jesus Christ of Latter-day Saints. The present cultural environment negatively impacts its ability to make and retain converts. The LDS Church claims that it is one of the fastest growing religions in the world,[8] but there are good reasons to doubt this. Although the noted sociologist of religion, Rodney Stark, boldly predicted that the LDS Church would reach 60 million by the year 2080, thus becoming the next major world religion to arise since Islam, Stark's thesis and his high growth rate projections have come under challenge.[9] In addition to questions about the growth rate for the LDS Church, serious questions have been raised about its ability to retain converts. According to the Mormon Social Science Association,[10] "retention rates of Mormon converts are very low,"[11] and this is borne out by survey and statistical data. Through a comparison of U.S. Mormon membership as reported by the Glenmary Research Center in contrast with the National Survey of Religious Identification and the American Religious Identification Survey, the Mormon Social Science Association concludes that [Mormonism] appears to attract a large number of converts ('in-switchers'), but also nearly as large a number of apostates ('out-switchers')."[12] Taking the best data sources into account, "[i]n sum, best estimates of retention

---

8 Rodney Stark, "The Rise of a new World Faith," *Review of Religious 26, no. 1* (September 1984): 18-27.

9 In terms of growth rate, see Gerald R. McDermott, "Testing Stark's Thesis: Is Mormonism the First New World Religion Since Islam?" in John W. Welch, ed., *The Worlds of Joseph Smith* (Provo: Brigham Young University Press, 2006), 271-92.

10 http://mormonsocialscience.org.

11 Mormon Social Science Association, "Ask an Expert: Retention Rates and Future Missionaries;" online document at http://www.mormonsocialscience.org/2008/10/09/q-retention-rates-and-future-missionaries/.

12 Ibid. Also see Peggy Fletcher Stack, "Keeping members a challenge for LDS church," *The Salt Lake Tribune (July 26, 2005)*: http://www.sltrib.com/ci_2890645; Joanna Brooks, "Mormon Numbers Not Adding Up," *Religion Dispatches (February 12, 2012)*: http://www.religiondispatches.org/archive/culture/5611/mormon_numbers_not_adding_up/.

rates for converts to Mormonism would probably put the number somewhere between 20% and 50%, depending on the country."[13] Even so, there is a bright spot from a Mormon perspective in that only 26% of Mormons are converts, and those born and raised in the faith are at a 70% retention rate (even if they are not necessarily active).[14]

LDS DISAFFILIATION AND MIGRATION

My purpose in referencing these numbers is to call attention to the reality of religious disaffiliation among Latter-day Saints, as well as the need for concern about the often-painful process of religious disaffiliation and migration. Each year thousands of people make the decision, for a variety of reasons, to exit the LDS Church in search of other options. To focus on one specific set of numbers, Richley Crapo calculated the U.S. LDS membership as of 2007.[15] His categories include membership inflows and outflows, attendance, and affiliations of the disengaged. Related to this essay, membership outflows (in terms of those who may choose a process of religious migration) included 63,224 disengaged nonbelievers (60.90%), 5,507 resignations (5.30%), and 3,333 excommunications (3.21%). In terms of religious migration destinations, Crapo includes these under the category of affiliations of the disengaged, with a breakdown of 26,554 (42.00%) choos-

13 Mormon Social Science Association, "Ask an Expert."

14 Pew Forum on Religion & Public Life/U.S. Religious Landscape Survey, "Chapter 2: Changes in Americans' Religious Affiliation." On the implications of this for Mormonism in contrast with other religious groups see J. Nelson-Seawright, "Mormonism is No Longer a Missionary Faith," By Common Consent blog (February 26, 2008): http://bycommonconsent.com/2008/02/26/mormonism-is-no-longer-a-missionary-faith/.

15 Available in an Excel file from the Mormon Social Science Association at http://www.MormonSocialScience.org/wp-content/uploads/2009/11/US-LDS-Membership-Balance-Sheet_0.xls.

ing nonbelief,[16] 21,496 (34.00%) choosing Protestantism, 13,909 (22.00%) choosing Roman Catholicism, and 1,264 (2.00%) choosing Eastern Orthodoxy.[17] In light of the number of people leaving Mormonism, and retaining some kind of interest in more traditional forms of Christianity, there is a need for resources that assist with this process of religious migration.

CONSIDERATIONS ON THE JOURNEY OF THE MORMON IMMIGRANT

Former Mormons face a number of challenges in their journey. One of the more insightful academic discussions of this process comes from Howard Bahr and Stan Albrecht in an essay that they wrote for the *Journal for the Scientific Study of Religion* in 1989.[18] In their discussion they frame religious migration in terms of "moving to a new country" and taking "citizenship in a new spiritual country."[19] With this imagery in mind, those who change churches or religious organizations may be likened to immigrants moving from one country to another. This religious migration involves a number of factors, and I will discuss highlights of these as discussed

---

16 This involves various forms of atheism and agnosticism. Crapo notes that this figure of 42% of total affiliations of the disengaged is "compared with 14% of out-conversions to nonbelief from other denominations."

17 In an earlier study "No preference," "Roman Catholic," and "Baptist, Born-Again Christian" are the leading three categories of religious preferences of former Mormons living in Utah in the 1980s. See Stan L. Albrecht and Howard M. Bahr, "Patterns of Religious Affiliation: A Study of Lifelong Mormons, Mormon Converts, and Former Mormons," in the *Journal for the Scientific Study of Religion 22, no. 4 (1983), 373.*

18 Howard M. Bahr and Stan L. Albrecht, "Strangers Once More: Patterns of Disaffiliation from Mormonism," *Journal for the Scientific Study of Religion 28, no. 2* (1989): 180-200. This study is dated, but it represents one of the few scientific studies available. Its age argues for the need to fund new research data for analysis.

19 Ibid., 180.

by Bahr and Albrecht. Although dated, their research is still helpful and relevant to the journey of contemporary religious immigrants.

In their research, Bahr and Albrecht drew upon two state-wide surveys in Utah among Latter-day Saints in the early 1980s and considered the results in light of their further research on religious disaffiliation, the creation of new roles of "ex" identity, and interviews with disaffiliates. Several aspects of their research are noteworthy, not only in what it tells us about religious disaffiliation from Mormonism, but also in the implications in assisting those in making the journey of religious reaffiliation.

First, a word of caution is in order. Due to the small number of interview subjects the authors consider their findings "exploratory and illustrative or sensitizing. They are not statistically generalizable in any way."[20] Further, they did "not attempt to generalize [their] findings to religious disaffiliates generally, or even to Mormon disaffiliates."[21] These statements reinforce the need for current and more expansive research done along these lines with a greater survey sample that will permit statistical generalizations so that we might further understand the process of religious disaffiliation among Latter-day Saints.

Second, Bahr and Albrecht draw upon the role theory work of Helen Ebaugh in her description of the "role-exit process" in a variety of relationship contexts.[22] She defines this as involving four stages that include "doubting one's role commitment, searching for viable alternative roles, experiencing a 'turning point' which reduces dissonance and mobilizes resources to exit, and creating an 'ex-role.'"[23] Ebaugh also includes discussion of how individuals come to grips with new roles for their lives, and how this relates to "ex-roles" and new senses of identity. Role theory and the four-part process of role-exiting in connection with identity theory provide a

---

20 Ibid., 187.
21 Ibid.
22 Helen Ebaugh, *Becoming an Ex: The Process of Role Exit* (Chicago and London: The University of Chicago Press, 1988).
23 Bahr and Albrecht, 185.

helpful framework and another significant facet for understanding the process of disaffiliation.

Third, the authors are cautious in the interpretation of disaffiliate accounts of prior group membership.[24] They remind us that

---

24 It is beyond the scope of this essay to critically examine the ex-Mormon narrative. On this see Albrecht and Bahr, "Patterns of Religious Disaffiliation:" 366-379; Stan L. Albrecht, Marie Cornwall and Perry H. Cunningham, "Religious Leave-Taking: Disengagement and Disaffiliation among Mormons," David G. Bromley, ed., *Falling from the Faith: Causes and Consequences of Religious Apostasy* (Newberry Park: SAGE Publications, 1988); Bahr and Albrecht, Strangers Once More,"; Seth R. Payne, "Purposeful Strangers: A Study of the ex-Mormon Narrative," Yale Divinity School (October 15, 2007); and Seth Payne and Ryan Wimmer, "Purposeful Strangers: Examining Ex-Mormons Narratives and Reasons People Give for Leaving the Church," Salt Lake City Sunstone Symposium presentation SL08374. The latter is especially significant in relation to evangelical approaches to Mormonism. This presentation touches on sociological studies in religious disaffiliation, secular anti-Mormon critiques of Mormonism, evangelical counter-cult critiques, and ex-Mormon narratives. Several aspects are noteworthy.

First, Payne and Wimmer note that no recent scientific survey work has been done to confirm why people leave the LDS Church or the religious or irreligious direction their lives take after their departure. This is significant in that evangelicals make statements about the effectiveness of apologetics aimed at "worldview annihilation" in regards to Mormons which then allegedly leads to migration into evangelical churches. Although some religious migration undoubtedly takes place in connection with apologetic exchanges, such claims as to why and the numbers of people involved in the process are anecdotal as scientific surveys have yet to be undertaken that can provide good data for a better understanding of the religious disaffiliation process in this context.

Second, Payne and Wimmer note that secular "anti-Mormon" critiques tend to be more prevalent than evangelical ones, and many of the secular arguments against Mormonism can be turned against traditional Christianity. For example, while evangelicals are quick to cite the "secular" argument of DNA against aspects of Book of Mormon genetics, many of the same scientists quoted in a popular apologetic video on this topic such accounts are "flawed" in that they "reflect only a single point of view - that of the disaffiliate - in a social process that involves scores, if not hundreds, of actors."[25] Further, Bahr and Albrecht note that the narratives of disaffiliates often "tend to interpret the past in ways that reduce personal dissonance about the decision taken. As a consequence, the perceptions of a typical former Mormon about an event are likely to be more anti-Mormon."[26] Yet even with these cautions concerning disaffiliate accounts the authors find value in them. They state that "the partiality of the observers is not reason to dismiss their reports as useless" since every human observer involves bias, "preconceptions and perceptual 'screens' which limit the scope and accuracy of his or her observations."[27] These considerations are helpful reminders of the need for caution in interpreting disaffiliate accounts, and that encounters with the many negative portrayals of Mormonism in evangelical literature

---

could argue against popular interpretations of the Genesis story in regards to human origins from a single historical human couple.

Third, Payne makes the important observation that while the General Authorities inform the faith of Latter-day Saints they do not dictate it. Thus, we should expect to find diversity and heterogeneity in Mormon faith and practice rather than the homogeneity often assumed by evangelicals on a popular level.

Fourth and finally, this presentation involved discussion of how ex-Mormon narratives take on a distinctive flavor that need to be studied by scholars carefully in order to understand them and the dynamics that inform them. Future survey research might benefit from the inclusion of how evangelical counter-cult depictions of Mormonism shape ex-Mormon concepts of Mormonism and the LDS Church.

It should also be noted that John Dehlin has launched a new research project and website called Why Mormons Leave, found at http://whymormonsleave.com/, which is designed to better understand the Mormon disaffiliation process. While interesting, it should be understood as anecdotal.

25 Bahr and Albrecht, 187.
26 Ibid., 188.
27 Ibid.

may help "color" disaffiliate accounts even further beyond the individual's experiences and perceptual reconstructions.

Fourth, the patterns and processes of disaffiliation are varied and complex. Bahr and Albrecht's research indicates that "[a]pparently most apostates from Mormonism were never truly 'in' the faith" in terms of being deeply devoted "fervent followers."[28] Most maintained marginal commitment levels of belief and identification. In terms of the disaffiliation of "fervent followers," while four out of six cited "intellectual defection" as a major part of their exiting process, the authors note that "[f]or even the most committed seeker, the intellectual struggle was only part of the process, since it occurred in a context of personal problems, disappointments and betrayals."[29] This feature of disaffiliation is a reminder that the process involves multiple factors of causation, and that intellectual as well as doctrinal and historical issues are processed and strongly influenced, for good or ill, within the important context of social relationships.

Finally, in the conclusion of the article one of the points raised by the authors is worth noting when they state:

It is also probable that patterns of disaffiliation observed among former Mormons in Utah are quite unrepresentative of former Mormons elsewhere. Both the dynamics of disaffiliation and the options of reaffiliation are likely to be quite different outside Utah, where Mormons do not represent the 'establishment' and typically are a small minority rather than the majority.[30]

Much more research needs to be done in order to develop a more complete understanding of the elements involved in the Mormon migration into a new spiritual country. But the work of Bahr and Albrecht, and others, provides important considerations and reminds us that religious migration is taking place. Just as an immigrant moving from one country to another faces a variety of

28 Ibid., 193.
29 Ibid., 197.
30 Ibid., 199.

challenges, so those making the journey of religious migration also face challenges as they shift from one religious culture to another. Culturally and religiously contextualized resources are needed to aid in this migration, and in the next section I will discuss *Transitions*,[31] a resource created to meet the specific needs of those migrating from Mormonism and into various Protestant expressions of Christianity.

TRANSITIONS: A UNIQUE RESOURCE FOR THE IMMIGRANT

Just as Mormons have recognized the need to create resources to assist those coming from more traditional forms of Christianity into Mormonism,[32] so evangelicals have also recognized the need to craft something to assist those coming from Mormonism and into traditional Christian churches. In response to the interests of pastors along the Wasatch Front, and having seen firsthand the struggles of former Mormon immigrants for many years, the staff of the Western Institute for Intercultural Studies made the decision to produce *Transitions* and to draw upon the metaphor of immigration in the facilitation of the journey. This is not the first resource created by evangelicals to assist former Mormons, but it is the first resource produced from the perspective of the person making the transition journey. Therefore *Transitions* makes a unique contribu-

---

31 *Transitions* can be previewed via a description, a trailer, the first video chapter, and the Introduction to the print workbook at http://www. LDStransitions.com. In addition, the entire video is available through Amazon Instant Video at http://tinyurl.com/ccm49aq. An extended version of the workbook with a narrative format involving former Mormons in each chapter is available in digital form at http://tinyurl.com/ d54arpb.

32 Elaine Cannon, *Beyond Baptism: A Guide for New Converts* (Salt Lake City: Bookcraft, 1994; and Clark L. and Kathryn H. Kidd, *A Convert's Guide to Mormon Life: A Guidebook for New Members of The Church of Jesus Christ of Latter-day Saints* (Salt Lake City: Bookcraft, 1998).

tion to resources by evangelicals addressing religious disaffiliation and reaffiliation in regards to Mormonism.[33]

The immigrant-oriented perspective of *Transitions* is significant and it was instrumental in the development of the material's structure as well as content. Other resources tend to approach the subject from the perspective of Protestant evangelicalism as the initial reference point. This perspective often begins from an inappropriate starting point in that it lends itself to gaps in providing what is needed in equipping the religious immigrant for the journey. For example, other resources often begin with significant evangelical doctrinal issues, such as biblical authority or trinitarian theology. As significant as these issues are for the evangelical, they do not resonate with the former Mormon. So by contrast, starting from the perspective of the immigrant, often experiencing pressing personal and emotional challenges, *Transitions* begins from this perspective and explores identity in chapter 1 of its video and workbook, and relationships in chapter 2. Our experience with former Latter-Day Saints has included many individuals who struggle with a sense of who they are, issues of personal identity that are now in doubt as a result of the severed ties to the LDS Church and the local ward. In addition, family struggles are unfortunately not uncommon, with relationships between husbands and wives, parents and children, grandparents and grandchildren fractured, and in some cases severed. The first two segments of *Transitions* provide insights to assist with the very real struggles that former

---

33 Indeed, most evangelical resources focus on evangelism or apologetic approaches with little thought given to the needs of religious reaffiliation and reinculturation in the local church. Other programs have been created by evangelical churches and parachurch organizations, but their approach is different. For example, the Institute for Religious Research promotes "Mormons in Transition" (http://mit.irr.org/) , but this follows an evangelical apologetic and theological template. *Transitions* breaks new ground in evangelical treatments of new religious movements with insights that are applicable to other evangelistic and discipleship contexts.

Mormon transitioners experience as they wrestle with new concepts of personal identity, and fractured or broken relationships.

The third segment involves discussion of church culture. This represents a significant evangelical blind spot, in that it is easy to take for granted what one experiences on a regular basis. Evangelicals are so immersed in evangelical church culture that it is easy to forget that former Mormons struggle with a variety of issues related to this new context, including things like clergy, church structure, means of service, stewardship, baptism, communion (LDS sacrament), places of service for men and women, and how to find a church home. The church culture segment of *Transitions* provides some important considerations for religious immigrants as they consider the many cultural differences between the local church and neighborhood ward.

It is only after addressing pressing personal issues that the second half of *Transitions* shifts to concerns related to doctrine and worldview. This segment is contextualized for former Latter-day Saints in two ways. First, recognizing the significance of the Mormon Plan of Salvation, it presents traditional Christian doctrine and worldview crafted in response to the three questions raised as part of this Mormon concept, including "Where did I come from?," "Why am I here?," and "Where am I going?." Second, the second half of *Transitions* presents traditional Christian teaching in narrative form as sacred story. The producers of *Transitions* recognize the cultural differences between traditional Christianity and Mormonism in that while the former has emphasized doctrine and systematic theology, the latter is not doctrinally-oriented.[34]

---

34 Evangelicals emphasize doctrine, orthodoxy, and a rational orientation to the theologizing process, but the Latter-day Saints do not. Most Latter-day Saints tend to emphasize ethics, a testimony, various sacred narratives, and ritual practices in the temple and ward. The sacred stories of Mormonism include items such as the Pre-Existence and the Heavenly Council, Joseph Smith's First Vision, and the Westward Trek and Persecution to name a few. These narratives represent not only theological and historical aspects of Mormonism, but also sacred stories in which

When issues of doctrine are considered it is more in terms of sacred story or narrative. Therefore, rather than presenting a list of doctrinal propositions which the former Mormon is expected to understand and assent to, *Transitions* presents the biblical narrative of God's Grand Story, His work of reconciliation from Genesis to Revelation.[35] Chapter four provides an overview of God's Story in six acts of the divine drama, which includes creation, catastrophe, covenant, Christ, church, and consummation.

Chapter five of *Transitions* takes up the question "Why am I here?," and helps the immigrant come to adopt a God-centered focus in service to God with a life of mission in self-giving love to others. The final chapter of *Transitions* addresses the question of "Where am I going?," and paints the broad strokes of an eschatology with an emphasis on God's restoration of all things and the complete establishment of the Kingdom of God.

Throughout the second section of *Transitions* where doctrine is presented an attempt was made to present a "mere Christianity," an

---

individual Latter-day Saints situate themselves as they seek identity and live out their faith individually and collectively. These stories are connected to strong experiential and emotional dimensions, which then work themselves out in ethical conduct and ritual that takes place in the home, ward, and temple.

35 This approach is exemplified in Christopher J. H. Wright, *The Mission of God: Unlocking the Bible's Grand Narrative* (Downers Grove: InterVarsity Press Academic, 2006). On narrative theology see George A. Lindbeck, *The Nature of Doctrine: Religion and Theology in a Postliberal Age* (Philadephia: Westminster Press, 1984); Timothy R. Phillips & Dennis L. Okholm, eds., *The Nature of Confession: Evangelicals & Postliberals in Conversation* (Downers Grove: InterVarsity Pres, 1996); Gabriel Fackre, *The Doctrine of Revelation: A Narrative Interpretation* (Edinburgh University Press, 1997); Stanley Hauerwas and L. Gregory Jones, eds., *Why Narrative? Readings in Narrative Theology* (Eugene; Wipf & Stock Publishers, 1997); George W. Stroup, *The Promise of Narrative Theology: Recovering the Gospel in the Church* (Eugene: Wipf & Stock Publishers, 1997); and Keith E. Yandell, ed., *Faith and Narrative* (New York: Oxford University Press, 2001).

expression of traditional Christian doctrine that would have appeal to a wide variety of Protestant, evangelical, charismatic, Pentecostal, and independent churches.

The response to *Transitions* has been very positive. It has been used by former Mormons in a number of states across America, with inquiries also coming from Europe, and requests being made that alternative versions of the material be made for the deaf community and in other languages for international use. One former Mormon exploring evangelicalism who used *Transitions* said, "If I would have had this resource when I first began my departure from Mormonism, it would have saved me years of struggle." This comment has been echoed in many of the responses we have received to *Transitions*.[36] In addition, when the material was presented to a gathering of non-traditional and liberal Mormons deeply committed to the Mormon worldview, positive statements were shared about the value of *Transitions*, and the potential for the high quality of the video production to touch the emotions perhaps even of committed Mormons.[37]

TRANSITIONS AND MULTIDISCIPLINARY BACKGROUND

A few more words might be said about another aspect of the uniqueness of *Transitions*, and that is its multidisciplinary background. Other resources designed for former Mormons draw upon theology and apologetics, as well as pastoral theology. *Transitions* draws upon these elements, but as mentioned above, even in the

---

36 Other comments from former Mormon immigrants about their journeys and how *Transitions* has helped can be found in Lisa Schencker, "The 'ex' factor: Videos help former Mormons find new faith," *The Salt Lake Tribune (June 22, 2012)*; http://www.sltrib.com/sltrib/life-style/54334211-80/church-evangelical-faith-latter.html.csp. Additional testimonials can also be read at http://www.ldstransitions.com/#!testi-monials/c22uh.

37 These were the reactions to this paper presented at Sunstone Symposium in Salt Lake City on July 29, 2012 on the campus of the University of Utah.

area of theology this resource provides a unique twist in its inclusion of narrative theology rather than systematic theology, and its minimal apologetic elements are contextualized and ancillary to the overall thrust of the resource. Beyond this, *Transitions* is also multidisciplinary in that it not only draws upon theology, but also upon identity theory, the process of role exit and new role formation, and the social scientific literature on religious disaffiliation and reaffiliation. Just as the process of disaffiliation and the ensuing journey of immigration are complex and multifaceted, so must be the response and the resources created to address these issues. The producers of *Transitions* recognized the need, and drew upon the sources necessary to serve as a background in crafting the resource to meet the challenges.

CONSIDERATIONS FOR RELIGIOUS INSTITUTIONS

As has been mentioned above, the process of leaving Mormonism and affiliating with a more traditional Christian church is a difficult and often painful process, as is the journey of migration from any religion to another. For whatever reasons, the history of animosity between Mormonism and Protestantism seems to exacerbate this process. Unfortunately, well-meaning individuals and institutions can make the process even more difficult, not only difficulties experienced from the LDS Church, but also those that arise in connection with in the new church affiliation.

Transitions was created to address these challenges, and it is the hope of the producers that the attempt to be fair representing Mormonism, in allowing the diversity of voices of former Mormons to speak for themselves, in creating a resource designed from the perspective of the religious immigrant, and in drawing upon a diversity of sources and disciplines for insights, that *Transitions* will continue to meet the needs many seekers. But beyond this, we also hope that *Transitions* can provide a helpful example for religious institutions in reducing the tensions and difficulties in the immigration journey, whether Mormon, evangelical, and beyond.

I I

The Second Greatest of These

STEVE DOUGLAS

Now these three things remain: faith, hope, and love; but the greatest of these is love. (1 Corinthians 13:13)

When people quote that verse, the odd man out is almost invariably hope.

Preachers and exegetes tend to read too much into serialized lists like the one there at the end of 1 Corinthians 13, imagining that everything listed has been presented by the author in a super-humanly insightful, divinely inspired order of importance. These people tend to turn those suppositions into sermons, or sometimes even entirely new doctrines, whereas as I tend to cast such speculations out as the fanciful effects of a too-mystical view of Scripture—of a sort that bears unmistakable affinities with the so-called Bible Code.

But in this case, I really can imagine that the order of "faith, hope, and love" was intentional after all. Paul certainly identifies the most important member of the group, which happens to be the last listed and could imply that the list is in order of "great, greater, greatest." This would mean that hope is next to love, and that faith, without which it is reportedly impossible to please God, is somehow not as "great" as hope. But could that be?

I don't honestly know if Paul meant to imply that gradation of importance; he certainly harped on faith a lot. But as far as I'm concerned, hope is at least as important as faith. And in one sense, it may be even greater.

What most Evangelicals refer to as faith is their adherence to a particular set of guiding beliefs and expectations. The lack of certainty is seen as the archenemy of faith. In removing the intrinsically unfulfilled aspect of hope from the equation, they are left with an understanding of faith as assumed certainty. But, as Paul once wrote, "Who hopes for what he already has?" We can live in anticipation, expectation, and even confidence of something without feigning certainty about it. It is those who force themselves to come to grips with the extremely tentative nature of our beliefs, ideals, and expectations who best understand the Christian hope and, as a result, faith.

The uncontested "greatest of these", love, is the basis of my faith and the object of my worship. Above all, it is in love that I trust and in whose interests I seek to act – the biblical understanding of "faith". I find a denial of the objectivity, universality, and absolute nature of love's existence and significance wholly unsatisfactory to my observation and experience, and I worship the Judeo-Christian God insofar as I believe He is Himself love personified. I believe that it is love in which we live, move, and have our being. So my faith is in love, specifically the sort described by followers of Jesus since the first century.

But this doesn't mean that hope is some strange third wheel. My faith – what I seek to live by – is motivated by my hope in love. In other words, faith is how I live, and hope is why I live that way. My commitment to living out my devotion to the absolute values of love and goodness is energized by my hopeful expectation that this kind of life will not be for naught. "Ain't no doubt in no one's mind that love's the finest thing around," as James Taylor put it, but it's hard to prove in any objective way. As much as we'd like to think otherwise, love's supreme value is not a given; the future may look upon us today with our enlightened ideals of love and indict this preoccupation as an unfortunate stumbling block in our race's evolution. But hope, which is essentially my refusal to give in to the fear of uncertainty, is what keeps me carrying on in the darkest days of doubt.

All the talk about the virtue of Christian doubt among the pro-gressive/liberal sort of Christians, myself included, understandably leaves many cold—again, myself included. Even while affirming the necessity of healthy skepticism, I have been discouraged to see a rising preoccupation with doubt among many of my fellow sojourners. Indeed, doubt has become the stereotypical post-Evan-gelical replacement for faith. As someone who closely studies the borderline between conservative and more progressive forms of Christianity on the Internet, I've witnessed several questioning Christians' blogs turning into doubt vs. faith zones, not necessarily because the authors really think that faith and doubt are opposites (although some probably do), but because in overcompensating for the problem of a steadfastly uninformed faith, they have for-gotten that doubt is not its own recipe, but merely an ingredient of a greater virtue, that "sunnier side of doubt" to which Tennyson alluded: hope.

Doubt is not a substitute for faith: it's a corrective measure for a faith characterized by artificial certitude. In leaving behind one's abusive relationship to religious certainty, it is all too easy to move in with religious doubt on the rebound, which, although comfort-ing at first, can eventually expose itself as an equally abusive – and harder to leave – form of certainty. Doubt has no positive existence worth celebrating; it is a side effect of humility, which begins in dis-comfort, settles into euphoria, but usually leaves those dwelling on it too long feeling hungry for more certainty. A healthy skepticism says, "I'll step lightly until I know this is true," whereas the un-healthy form of it I see too much of these days says, "I'll go around looking for things to debunk, and stand on whatever's left." Al-though the widespread misunderstanding of faith as blind belief among Evangelicals is legitimately critiqued by a humble recogni-tion of our fallibility and potential for self-delusion, this deficiency is not necessarily remedied by either a similarly conceived disbelief or a similarly blind default stance of skepticism. When certainty eludes us, we must avoid manufacturing it in any direction; I am suggesting we would do well to remember the under-appreciated virtue of hope.

Rather than maintaining difficult-to-accept beliefs, our faith is about fervently striving to bring the Goodness we have known closer to the waiting world. While valuing the insights into the human and divine natures the biblical authors have to offer us, and while humbly and thoroughly subjecting those insights to all of the reconstructions and deconstructions suggested by critical inquiry, we do not lean on either understanding. We trust instead in the God for whom our souls yearn and without whom all the truths on the earth would be nothing more than clanging cymbals. Our faith is realized in an ethic intended to make those virtues manifest in our own lives, for the sake of others: we demonstrate our hope for the victory of love by acting faithfully, seeking to embody goodness, beauty, justice, meaning, and above all, love. This is what we call serving God. We are Christians because we were – and are – taught these things by Jesus.

My hope, more than my credulity, is in the Christian God. Do I believe in God, Jesus, the ethic of love articulated by my forbears in the Christian faith, etc.? In a sense, but primarily because I hope in them. Hope steers my faith, not the assumption of certainty that masquerades as faith. My theological speculations are explanations of how I expect my hope to be realized by Love's final victory; my faith is merely how I go about fulfilling my theology. My hope is my soul's response to Love, the impulse by which I commit to exercise my life of faith. It seems to me, then, that this faith-generative aspect of hope makes it much closer to love than faith is.

Not recognizing a reasoned, conscious hope as an alternative to the make-believe of those in stout denial of reality, many who have come down this road with me have decided that they are content to rest in disbelief, a ready shelter from the turmoil of doubt. To be sure, getting one's head out of the clouds and finding the beauty where we are on the ground is a laudable task, and I will listen to what they teach me and respectfully wish them well; but hope calls me deeper.

This talk of absolutes and ultimates is, of course, quite unpopular, especially among us post-Evangelical post-modernists. "Who made the absolutes? Well then, who made the maker of the absolutes?" And it's true: we can't absolutize everything we happen to believe. But despite this challenge of infinite regress, I steadfastly abide in the hope that way, way down there, below all those turtles, Love lies as the ground of all being. The moment we begin our exploration of the expanse beyond the turtle upon which our world sits, we become like strangers in a strange land. Hope is my motivation to step out of my capsule of unquestioned certainty and into that unknown world, knowing full well that what I inhale there may have tragic consequences for my well-being. I proceed because, after all, the air where I'm headed can hardly be any more unhealthy than the air I'm leaving behind. So many people bending over backwards to shame me into agreeing that this world has "at bottom, no design, no purpose, no evil and no good, nothing but blind, pitiless indifference" – it's either stay and suffocate while I try to convince myself to be satisfied in this world of only ad hoc meaning or dare to suppose that my difficulty in breathing where I am is due to the fact that, in Lewis's words, "I was made for another world." I will embrace even the faint opportunity to fill my lungs with a purer air, to finally reach that ground of being that has beckoned my soul, so that I may at last find true peace and be able to offer it to this hurting world.

So in my hope in a love still largely unrealized, I take a deep breath, step out, and place my foot on the back of the next turtle down … and just hope that it's not a snapping turtle.

12

GRACE: IT'S NOT JUST FOR DINNER

These souls whom God is beginning to lead through these solitary places of the wilderness are like to the children of Israel, to whom in the wilderness God began to give food from Heaven, containing within itself all sweetness, and, as is there said, it turned to the savour which each one of them desired.

TRAVIS MILAM

Ephesians 2:8-10

Hi, my name is Travis and I am a legalist. This is something I never dreamed that I would be standing here and admitting to all of you. You see, I have known what the Bible says about grace and works and I have never doubted that I have been saved by grace. I would tell you how God saved me and how I was a better person for it and that all you needed to do was see how my life showed this. I did not drink, do drugs, curse, or use tobacco. I listened to my parents and elders and never questioned authority. I knew my Bible and I knew all the answers. All you had to do was just ask. I could prove it by quoting scripture, quoting doctrine, and I had the awards and esteem of others to show it. In short, I had become what I claimed I despised: a legalist who depended upon my works to prove that I was right with God.

When I realized what I had become, I knew I had to do something to change. So I have created a new program which I have named Legalists Anonymous or LA for short. There are only three steps to this program, but don't be fooled into thinking they are easy. By no means are they easy. These steps are as follows: 1. Admit what you are, 2. Commit to change, and 3. Remember what you were and extend grace to others. Let us take some time now to examine each step.

Admission is always the hardest step. As with other programs similar to this one, you have to admit you have a problem. Many do not see that they have a problem. To them, others have the problem. If only those who "have a problem" would just be like me, they say, then they would know what a proper relationship with God is like. I know, I had, and still have, the problem of legalism. I was, and still am, a legalist. I say I still am because like many addictions, there is always the possibility of falling back into the cycle of legalism.

Growing up I attended VBS and repeated memory verses, participated in sword drills, and stood out because I was always one of the top participants. I chose the prizes that would make me look good in others' eyes, not because I wanted to grow closer to God. I had my reward in that others saw me as a good person, a good Christian person, who had all that God wanted a person to be. Sure, I might watch some TV or movies or listen to songs that weren't quite on the same standard, but hey, I was saved by grace and I knew where I was going, did you? In other words, I was a self righteous hypocrite and I fed on what I was taught. See, we talked about grace at church, but we held to rules that governed what a good person could be. It was like we were singing Amazing Grace in this way, "Amazing grace, how sweet the sound that saved a wretch like me. I once was lost but now am found. Was blind but now I see … that list of rules that will keep me in line with God and will make sure I don't get in his bad favor." I like this. I told myself I had no problem. I was what God wanted.

Then I went to college and began to see what other people were like. They did not follow the rules I did. Some men had long hair, earrings and wore jewelry besides a wedding band or class ring. They listened to music that was suspiciously like pop or rock music. They were friends with people who were questionable (in my eyes) in morals because they may have drunk alcohol or smoked. And yet, they knew their Bibles better than I. They were not nearly as uptight as I was. They lived what they said they believed. They taught grace. And I wanted that. I first had to admit what I was. That was one of the hardest things I ever had to do, but when I did, I knew that I had started the road to recovery.

Committing to change from legalism is not easy, as I quickly discovered. I had to accept people as they were, not as I believed they should be. I had to understand that Paul was speaking to me when he wrote to the Galatians asking who took their freedom and that for freedom Christ had set me free. No longer was I under the yoke of working to prove my relationship with God. I had always tried to show that I was free by doing things I thought people needed to see, not be the person God wanted. I did what I did because I wanted praise. I was the Pharisee that I despised.

I knew Ephesians 2:8-10. I knew that works would not get me to heaven. I knew it was by grace I was saved. So why did I work so hard? Because in my eyes and how I was taught, you always wanted the outward signs. But deep inside I knew that I was still a prisoner to the law and not free by grace. It was like a story I had heard of Frederick the Great. Frederick was known as an enlightened ruler for his time and he wanted to see how his prisons operated and see how the inmates were treated. He began his tour with the warden and was met by the inmates, knowing that one word from Frederick could free them, proclaiming their innocence, all the while rattling the chains that held them. As he continued his tour Frederick came to one cell where the inmate would not even look at the king. Frederick asked, "Do you know who I am?" The man answered, "Your majesty, I know who you are and I am not fit to look upon your face. I am guilty as charged and deserve the punishment that was handed down." Upon hearing this, Frederick turned to the warden and said, "Get this man out of here before he corrupts all these innocents!"

We may laugh, but isn't that what we are and isn't that what Christ has done for us? When we admit we can do nothing to make ourselves better, we are set free from trying. But then, many of us turn around and begin to try to earn that freedom that has been freely given! It is like we don't want to face that fact that we can do nothing to earn grace and by golly, we are going to make sure others know that as well.

When I finally committed to grace, a huge weight was lifted. I realized I no longer had to be the best at the Christian life. I no longer had to worry if another thought of me as sinful because of what I did. I was free in Christ. Now I realize that I was not given license to do what I wanted. Even Paul says we are not to go about doing whatever wily nilly. But I also realized that I had wasted a good deal of my freedom worrying about what others had thought of me and I committed to never waste it again.

Remembering from whence you came is also very hard. But it is vital to living grace and not falling back into legalism. Indulge me one more story. It is from Victor Hugo's *Les Miserables*. In the story Jean Valjean has been released from prison and, after no one else would, is taken in for the night by a kind bishop and his sister. During the night, Valjean steals the family silver and flees. The next day he is brought back by the police who have captured him and is most certainly going to prison for the rest of his life. However, the bishop does something extraordinary. He expresses delight that Valjean has returned and admonishes him that he forgot the candlesticks. He informs the police that the silver was a gift and Valjean is left with the old man. The bishop then gives him the candlesticks saying, "Do not forget, do not ever forget that you have promised me to use the money to make yourself an honest man." Valjean, having been given the gift of grace, keeps the candlesticks as a memento and dedicates himself to helping others in need.

Remembering is not just for us. Yes, we must remember where we have been and where we are going. To forget would be an injustice to the grace we have been given. But we must also reach out to others as well. In remembering, we must show that grace has been given to them as well. In helping others, we must never recall the past to use as guilt and shame. What has been repented and forgiven by God must be forgiven by us as well. We are called to bear one another's burdens and not press down what is in the past.

Far too often we want to make sure someone remembers what he or she has done. Do you not think they know? I have often said that the church is a hospital for sinners and we are very good at shooting our wounded. Reach out a helping hand and pick up those who are down, dust them off and take the journey with them remembering that you too once needed grace to be where you are.

I realize that these three steps are big steps for many of us. Admitting, Committing and Remembering are things that take time and effort. But when we do so these steps will change our lives in ways we have never imagined. A line from a song says, "If the Son has set you free, you are free indeed." Why go back to prison when freedom beckons? You see, grace is not just for dinner, but to be lived.

13

A JOURNEY THROUGH THE SPIRITUAL NIGHT

I remained, lost in oblivion; My face I reclined on the Beloved. All ceased and I abandoned myself, Leaving my cares forgotten among the lilies.

CRAIG FALVO[1]

In some circles of Christianity, the mere mention of the word "doubt" is enough to draw awkward glances from across the room. To put it simply, doubt is something a great deal of Christians experience, but something very few of us like to discuss. When doubt is discussed, it is often done in hushed, confused voices. And most importantly, quite often, doubt hurts. Theologian and apologist Alister McGrath writes:

> It's surprising how many Christians prefer not to talk about doubt. Some even refuse to think about it. Somehow, admitting to doubt seems to amount to insulting God, calling his integrity into question. It is quite understandable that you might feel this way about doubt: on the one hand, you may thing that admitting to doubt is a sign of spiritual or intellectual weakness; on the other, you may be reluctant to admit those doubts to your friends, in case you upset them, perhaps damaging their own faith.[2]

In my opinion, this is where Christians go wrong in their dealing with doubt. Because of this aversion to even discussing or

---

1 theonerd.com

2 Alister McGrath, *Doubting*, (Downers Grove: InterVarsity Press, 2006), 13.

in the most extreme instances, failing to even think about doubt, there is a lot of misunderstanding as to the role doubt can play in the spiritual life of a believer.

As someone who has worked through the hurt and the stigma associated with doubt, I want to share my descent into doubt and how the journey from doubt to faith changed me theologically.

The first thing that we need is an understanding of doubt, what it is and what it is not. McGrath states:

> In the first place, doubt is not skepticism - the decision to doubt everything deliberately, as a matter of principle.
>
> In the second, it's not unbelief - the decision not have have faith in God. Unbelief is an act of will, rather than a difficulty in understanding.[3]

The doubt that I want to discuss is also not what Robert N. Wennberg calls theoretical doubt, "a kind of intellectual puzzlement or questioning."[4] What I mean by doubt is what Wennberg calls existential doubt, a doubt that is:

> very personal and reply disturbing, famously called "the dark night of the soul" by the Christian mystic Saint John of the Cross. There are times - many or few, long or short - when God seems remote, when one doesn't feel God's presence in one's life, when God is experientially absent, when his very existence seems uncertain, when everything one believes as a Christian is called into serious question.[5]

Now that we have a better understanding spiritual doubt, I would like to share my story of doubt. The descent into doubt began in early January 2011. I was working at a Lutheran Church in the Seattle area as their Director of Child, Youth, and Family

---

3 *Ibid.*, 13-14.
4 Robert N. Wennberg, *Faith at the Edge: A Book for Doubters,* (Grand Rapids: Wm. B. Eerdmans Publishing Co., 2009), 3-4.
5 *Ibid.*, xv-xvi

Ministries. My wife and I had moved out to Seattle in 2009 after I graduated from seminary for this position. My wife gave up a job in her field working for the city of Columbia, SC on the hope that I would be able to finish my Diaconal Ministry project and become consecrated as a Diaconal Minister in the Evangelical Lutheran Church in America (ELCA).

This church had a rather large staff for it's size: two full time pastors, a three-quarter time administrator, a variety of stipend positions and my position. During my first year of ministry at the church, one of the pastors was on leave from his call there and his absence helped the church to meet it's budget, for a time. During that year the church experienced no positive growth. In fact, as to be expected in a church where their average age is 65, the church lost a few members. There was also the recession to contend with. Negative growth and lower giving put in motion the events that would lead to my journey into the dark night.

I was already unhappy in the position and it was in January that things moved from bad to worse. The "budget" (I use the term loosely, the church had a spending guide, not a true budget) talks were not going well and the estimated shortfall was more than the church could handle. Something drastic had to be done. The first step was more of a short term fix, cut salaries for the first half of the year. While not ideal, we were able to get by on the decrease in my salary.

In the middle of March, my biggest fear was confirmed. Out of what I perceived to be panic, fear, and reaction, the Personnel Committee made the recommendation to eliminate my position, not because I was doing a bad job, but because they "wanted" two pastors and assumed that one of the pastors could do my job on top of his. At least that's what they said openly. My perception, looking back on this after a year and half, is that they did not want to retire the 65 year old pastor who had been there for twenty plus years. Needless to say, I was angry and bitter at a church which, in my opinion, was not acting like the church. And, I was angry and bitter at God. I questioned how a loving God, in his infinite knowledge, could allow me move my family out to Seattle, only to be abandoned by the church I was working for.

In April 2011, a few weeks after being told my position was being eliminated, I spent a weekend at Holden Village, a retreat center in the mountains near Chelan, Washington. This weekend was supposed to be a retreat for a few senior high students. But over the course of registering to the time of the actual retreat, all of the senior high students backed out. On the advice of the Associate Pastor and with the consent of the group holding the retreat, I still went up to Holden for the three day retreat. Now, Holden Village is a remote retreat center. To get there, one must take an hour long ferry ride over Lake Chelan and then take a twenty to thirty minute bus ride up into the mountains. Holden is so remote that there is no cell phone service and they make their own electricity. Knowing this, I left my laptop and iPad at home and took a few books to read. But little did I know that one of these books would be the catalyst for my journey through doubt to faith.

The trip up to Holden was uneventful. After waking up early, I drove four hours from Seattle to Chelan where I was to meet the ferry. Even the ferry ride and the drive up the mountain were, for all intents and purposes, as one would expect (this is excluding the silliness that was put on by the staff of Holden on the drive up). After arriving at Holden and getting the feel for the weekend, I got my suitcase up into my room and promptly fell asleep and didn't wake up until after dinner had already been served.

The first memorable moment of the weekend happened after I woke up from my extended nap, something I very much needed. I scavenged some food, mainly bread and tea, went back up to my room and began to read *The Nature of Love: A Theology* by Thomas Jay Oord. At this point in my personal theology, I was on the fence concerning open theism. I had read *The Openness of God* by Clark Pinnock, but wasn't really sold on the whole idea. But, with what I was going through personally, I think that this particular weekend I was more open to different answers than traditional theology was providing me. It took me the rest of that first night and most of the next day to read through Oord's book. After reading that book during that weekend, I could no longer hold to a traditional view of God's foreknowledge or God's knowledge of the future. A shift in my theology needed to happen.

The other memorable moment happened during Sunday's worship, when there was a a period of prayer. In my typical style, I was late, so I'm not sure if I missed something at the beginning, but during the period of prayer, people would go up to a box filled with sand, light a candle and place it in the sand. As I was watching, I noticed that periodically, a group of people would go up and lay hands on someone who was praying; however, I didn't think anything of it. Now keep in mind that I'm not one who easily picks up on subtlety. What I didn't notice was that there were two different shapes for the boxes to place the candle in; one square and one circle. And when people would go to one of the shapes, others would join them. So, I went to the closest one and was amazed when people came up and laid hands on me. Amazed is an understatement. I still remember thinking, "How did all those people know I needed prayer?" I actually didn't find out about the differences in the shape of the boxes until the day I left. Turns out that I just happened to pick the shape that was a cue to others to come up and join me. Though due in part to missed information, it was still a powerful moment that left me stunned.

I often remind myself that these two events were exactly what I needed to begin my journey through doubt. I needed to know there was other ways of thinking about God's knowledge and I needed to know that I was not going through this alone. I needed to feel God's presence in my life. And, like Thomas, I needed proof in order to begin the move from doubt to faith. The rest of the weekend was uneventful. I had a few forgettable conversations. But those two events became the catalyst for my journey though doubt.

Don't get me wrong, I wasn't cured of my doubt during this weekend. It has taken time and theological reflection. In some ways, my journey through the dark night is still ongoing. Some of the negative feelings from the experience still haunt me and it is something that will be with me for a while. My journey through doubt was one wrought with pain and tears and fear of the unknown. Journeying through was just as painful, if not more so, than journeying into doubt. My journey through doubt to faith has also been a journey filled with prayer, conversation, and rediscovery. Over the past year, I have grown closer with several people, both in my church community and in the blogosphere as I have shared and reflected on my journey through doubt. I have rediscovered my love for theology and have been reading works I have previously ignored, such as *Dark Night of the Soul* by St. John of the Cross.

Most importantly, it has been a journey of letting go. I've had to let go of a lot over the past year and half. I've let go of my anger and bitterness, at least toward God. I've let go of my fear and my hurt. I have weathered one dark night and come out on the other side with my faith intact. My doubt does not have control of me anymore.

Finally, I want to leave you with this: Doubt is not something new to Christianity or to believers. We can see examples of doubt all through out the Bible and in those who have gone before us in the faith. One of the best examples I can think of from the Bible happens shortly after the Resurrection. For those of us who use the lectionary, we hear this story of doubt on the Second Sunday of Easter.

> It was still the first day of the week. That evening, while the disciples were behind closed doors because they were afraid of the Jewish authorities, Jesus came and stood among them. He said, "Peace be with you." After he said this, he showed them his hands and his side. When the disciples saw the Lord, they were filled with joy. Jesus said to them again, "Peace be with you. As the Father sent me, so I am sending you." Then he breathed on them and said, "Receive the Holy Spirit. If you forgive anyone's sins, they are forgiven; if you don't forgive them, they aren't forgiven."
>
> Thomas, the one called Didymus, one of the Twelve, wasn't with the disciples when Jesus came. The other disciples

told him, "We've seen the Lord!" But he replied, "Unless I see the nail marks in his hands, put my finger in the wounds left by the nails, and put my hand into his side, I won't believe." After eight days his disciples were again in a house and Thomas was with them. Even though the doors were locked, Jesus entered and stood among them. He said, "Peace be with you." Then he said to Thomas, "Put your finger here. Look at my hands. Put your hand into my side. No more disbelief. Believe!" Thomas responded to Jesus, "My Lord and my God!" Jesus replied, "Do you believe because you see me? Happy are those who don't see and yet believe." Then Jesus did many other miraculous signs in his disciples' presence, signs that aren't recorded in this scroll. But these things are written so that you will believe that Jesus is the Christ, God's Son, and that believing, you will have life in his name.[6]

The text begins when it was evening on that day, the day of the resurrection. It was hours ago that Mary Magdalene had gone to the tomb and found that it was empty. And now, on that very same day, Jesus appears to the disciples for the first time. The disciples are locked away in a room, afraid, even though just a few hours ago, Mary had proclaimed to them that she had seen the risen Lord. Suddenly, Jesus appears in the midst of them. But notice, no one recognizes Jesus until he shows them the wounds. Jesus then breaths the Holy Spirit into the disciples. By breathing the Holy Spirit into the disciples, Jesus gives them a new life. There is also a close connection between the giving of the Holy Spirit and the sending of the disciples. It is the Spirit that consecrates the disciples so that they are consecrated as Jesus was consecrated during his baptism, that they can be sent as Jesus was sent by God. When Jesus gives the disciples the Holy Spirit, he enables them to carry on his mission, the same mission that we are enabled to do today. Jesus gives the disciples the Holy Spirit, just as he gives us the same Holy Spirit during our baptism.

We find out that one of the disciples was not there. Thomas was not with the rest of the disciples on that first Easter evening.

---

6   John 20:19-31, Common English Bible

He had missed out on the first appearance of Jesus. We are not told why Thomas was not there with the rest of the disciples, we are only told of his absence. Thomas is told by the rest of the disciples that Jesus has risen from the dead, that Jesus is alive. Thomas wants proof, "Unless I see the nail marks in his hands, put my finger in the wounds left by the nails, and put my hand into his side, I won't believe."[7] This response by Thomas has earned him a bad reputation, that of a doubter. But Thomas wasn't the only one who did not believe that Jesus had been raised from the dead. Earlier in John 20, Mary stood outside the tomb, weeping. She sees two angels of the Lord and they want to know why she is crying. Mary responds, "They have taken away my Lord, and I don't know where they've put him."[8] Mary did not believe that Jesus had been raised from the dead, she thought that someone had moved the body. And even when she is approached by Jesus, she does not recognize him. It is only after Jesus speaks her name does she recognize Jesus. It is important to note that the disciples use the exact same announcement to Thomas that Mary spoke to the disciples on that first Easter morning, "We have seen the Lord!"[9] The very same announcement given to the disciple hours before they go into hiding.

But in reality, this is not a story about doubt. This is not even a story about Thomas. This is a story about Jesus. Here we have an offer made by Jesus to Thomas, the offer to touch the wounds. Jesus is not attempting to embarrass or shame Thomas for not believing the disciples proclamation. Jesus is giving Thomas exactly what he needs for faith. Upon seeing the wounds, Thomas responds, "My Lord and my God!"[10] Thomas sees God fully revealed in Jesus. Thomas is not rebuked by Jesus for needing to see to believe. Rather, Jesus gives Thomas a sign and asks him to believe. "Put your finger here. Look at my hands. Put your hand into my side.

---

7 John 20:24, CEB
8 John 20:13, CEB
9 John 20:24, CEB
10 John 20:28, CEB

No more disbelief. Believe!"[11] Jesus gives Thomas exactly what he needs to overcome his doubt. Then, Jesus makes a promise. "Blessed are those who have not seen and yet have come to believe." Jesus' care for the faith of those who come after Thomas, who will not and cannot see the wounds, is equally without limit or measure. Through God's grace, we too are recipients of this pledge and promise. Through God's grace and by the power of the Holy Spirit, we are able to have faith and believe without seeing. And by God's grace, Christ gives us exactly what we need to overcome our doubt.

Works Cited

McGrath, Alister. *Doubting*. Downers Grove: InterVarsity Press, 2006.

Wennberg, Robert N. *Faith at the Edge: A Book for Doubters*. Grand Rapids: Wm. B. Eerdmans Publishing Co., 2009.

---

11 John 20:27, CEB

14

My Road to Freedom

Doug Jantz

My journey to, and with, faith has been a long one, not unlike many others I am sure. I say 'with' because I don't think I would have come this far without it. Weak though faith is at times it is all we really have, isn't it?

I grew up in the non-instrumental Churches of Christ. Most were very conservative according to my memory. Filled with loving people, though. No matter which congregation they were all mostly identical. Service times, the way the assemblies were ordered, things that were taught, the way things were done were all pretty much uniform across all of them.

The Bible was of interest to me at a very young age and to this I credit these churches and those who taught and preached. I remember living in Hardy, Arkansas while in second grade and finding Hurlbut's *Story of the Bible* on a shelf in the hallway at home. The book fascinated me, filled with pictures and stories in a way I could read them. The funny thing is no one ever told me to read this book or any others, I just did.

At 7 years old I received my first Bible from my parents, the King James version, which was about all we had then. It is still in my possession and when I look through it I see notes I wrote in places even at this young age. I loved reading it and asking questions in Sunday School.

I learned the importance of Bible study and the story contained in it. For this I am thankful. Church was something I never found to be a burden, always enjoying it and going every time I could. In Arkansas when I was in second grade tent meetings were popular in the Churches of Christ, for days at a time. We would go at night, sometimes for two weeks solid.

I remember one such meeting in particular with Charles Coil preaching. My mom tells me I was fascinated listening to him. Years later I met and talked with him and told him I remembered him preaching then. The main goal of these was to evangelize those who we considered to be lost, away from God, to bring them to faith, repentance and to baptize them.

So evangelism was familiar to me since a young child. Other preaching was done comparing the Churches of Christ to denominations, convincing people they were in the wrong churches and needed to obey the "pattern" set forth by God in scripture. The hermeneutic used was that the "pattern" could be seen by 3 things: command, example, and necessary inference.

This is how I saw everything about scripture. Not as a collection of writings by people of faith telling of their experiences with God, but as a rulebook for life. Things to do and not to do. The things to do kept me in the good graces of God and the rest, well, those put me over the sinner line. Those would cause God to no longer favor me or bless me.

I went to Church of Christ schools, starting with college. A college that measured our hair to keep it from going below our ears, nor were we allowed beards. But again, some good Bible scholars were my professors and I will always be grateful for that. Literalness was the normal teaching but the text was taught. I had to read the text and learned it even better, though not the heart of the meaning behind it.

This is the time I decided I wanted to preach and someday teach as well. I enrolled in the Harvard of preaching schools among Churches of Christ and was accepted. Sunset School of Preaching in Lubbock, Texas was considered the best with the best expository preachers anywhere. Support was required to be in school as there was no time for outside work. A normal course of teaching crammed into two years. Never before had I read, studied and memorized so much scripture.

I loved my time there, learning to study and to preach what I had learned, even though I thought I would fail Greek! Again, study and learning was drilled into my head. We were required to go on door knocking campaigns during some of our break weeks. The purpose again was evangelism and to invite people to come hear the true gospel preached, to learn the differences in churches and to become a "member" of our group.

This all taught me a lot, though. Talking to total strangers is an art form and we learned it and were taught it in classes, not unlike Mormons, Jehovah Witnesses and other groups who still do this today. I had all the answers to any questions that could be asked and a checklist to go through to bring the person "to Christ" so that they might be saved. Just like a sales pitch, for this is what it was. Questions and answers designed to lead the person to an inevitable conclusion, which required a yes or no answer. Baptisms or "conversions" were usually of a great number during these campaigns and great rejoicing was done over them. After all, another soul was saved and had been brought into the one, true church.

For several years I remained in Churches of Christ as Youth Minister and Sr Minister. The start of my turning was some research into the issue of instrumental music, which for me was a major thing. Those who don't grow up with this cannot understand it. I wrote scholars who had helped translate various versions and compiled tons of notes and my own research. My conclusion was that the arguments were invalid and the whole thing was a moot point.

From here I moved to Sr Minister with an Independent Christian Church, one which was quite liberal where I was given a lot of latitude in my study, teaching and preaching. Fresh air! But, something was still missing with me. My impression was that all I had done was change denominations. Everything else seemed the same. I left the congregation amidst some other issues and haven't stepped into a pulpit since. But my studying continued off and on.

I took some classes at Missouri State University in Springfield, Missouri. One was World Religions, which I did not have any interest in. That soon changed and opened up a new world to me. I learned that other religions seemed to have some things similar to what I had grown up with. Then I took a class on historical theology and learned that my particular church had not indeed been the first, original church from the beginning. We came a LOT later. As I look back on a lot of this I am astounded how blinded we are in our own individual religious groups. When I describe this to others they just stare at me, unable to understand what I always took as THE truth.

A very big eye opener came as I was studying through Marti Steussy's *David: Portraits of Biblical Power*. I saw things I had not been able to see earlier, that texts do contradict, writers do present God in different ways, and even more. Why had I not been able to see this before? What about inspiration? Didn't that guarantee the writers wrote God's words to them verbatim? If differences did indeed exist in the texts, even contradictions, what else had I believed in that was not true?

I was actually very distraught over this. What I had based my trust on was not true after all. For months I was lost and had no idea where to go with any of this. I sought counsel from Marti Steussy who directed me to Dr James Barr, who was gracious enough to help me think things through by email. This was a very difficult period for me to get through, but I did. I spoke to Dr Stanley Burgess about this after a course with him at Missouri State University and he told me he was surprised I had gotten through it by myself and that some of his students had to have counseling over this very thing.

I began attending a Disciples of Christ congregation and found it refreshing. Much different than that with which I had grown up. Yet it still felt like the same song with a different verse. Still I kept looking. To this day I have no idea where I fit in, feeling too liberal for conservatives and too conservative for real liberals.

The last couple of years I have done more reading and planning to enter classes once again. I feel more comfortable in my thinking now though I feel as if I know nothing compared to how I used to feel! What I DO know is that I no longer have to feel as if I know all the answers. I am OK with this. I have more questions now than ever but I keep going, trying to figure things out each day. I have run the gamut of questioning the existence of a God or god(s) to thinking there is a God to not even sure day to day.

To this day I still wonder almost every day the point of it all. Inspiration means more than it did before and means so much in different ways. God is at work in everyone, if indeed God is there. The work and creating is not limited to me or certain groups of people or religions.

The Hebrew and Christian Scriptures mean more to me than ever before. The records of the experiences people had with God and the meanings they saw in them are a wonder to read. Literal? Not at all, but so full of truths for us all. I think this is continuing through us now, though I don't know how or where it is happening. Again, I am ok with this!

I no longer fear what I don't know. My faith is secure no matter what and I actually feel so much more free not knowing all the answers. Indeed, there may not even be answers as we have been led to think of them. They may change in each generation depending on us and what our situations are.

15

UNSETTLED CHRISTIANITY

Oh, night that guided me, Oh, night more lovely than the dawn, Oh, night that joined Beloved with lover, Lover transformed in the Beloved!

JOEL L. WATTS[1]

There is a hesitancy in describing the gore of my internal hemorrhage. At first, when I spoke about it, I would more often than not speak in hushed tones, wondering if I would, at that very moment, break. When I first approached the publisher with this idea, I felt like I could easily write my story to the benefit of others. Both my wife and my counselor had at one time or another suggested that I write these experiences out for a variety of reasons, one of them, of course, to serve as self-healing. In the final preparations for this book, I was the last one to finish the manuscript because I have found that it is still difficult to speak — to speak about and out. In what follows, I have purposely avoiding any heavy editing and instead hope to produce some of the chaos many of us are in as we face such a difficult transition.

Maybe I should start at the end, to relieve you of any undue emotion. But I'm not sure I know where the end is. I can tell you that I am currently a Sunday School teacher in a local United Methodist Church. I have a different set of friends now. Overall, my life is better. Of course, I know that I am still not on a completely solid emotional foundation — after all, it has taken me this long to explore my story, for myself. As much as this current end draws me, let me start somewhere near the beginning.

---

1 unsettledchristianity.com

In 33 C.E. a Jewish fellow died on a cross because we are told he sought to bring hope to the oppressed, the sinners, and the Gentiles; he died because he was inclusionary. Within two generations, a new sect had emerged that proclaimed the God of the Jews as the universal God who equally loved the Gentiles. In the fourth century, the final break occurred that would lead to bloodshed, wars, and fierce hatred. Over the course of the centuries, what had become a Church became several churches. These several churches split to become denominations and these denominations would see breakaway sects erupt. In the latter third of the second millennium after the birth of Jesus, an English man by the name of John Wesley saved the Protestant Reformation from descending into useless oblivion when he set about to appeal to the common people, charting a course back to heavy theology.

His method moved to the colonial frontier where it took hold in the form of what we call pentecostalism. This virulent form of charismatic Christianity eventually separated itself from the older denominations, but resided still in the American frontier. Fire and brimstone were mixed with the shouts and other-worldly language assumed to be that of angels. Education was eschewed as was organizational structures. Wesley's wise focus on Tradition was expelled without good reason, leading only to an experience-based scripture reading. Pentecostalism, still orthodox in that it accepted the Trinity and a few other normative Christian doctrines, grew until the early part of the last century in the second millennium. During this time, anti-educated pentecostals decided that the Trinity, a doctrine sacred to Christians since at least the second century, was a sign of the corruption Rome had placed upon the Church. Thus, the oneness movement was born.

We are not yet were we need to be.

At some point before 1921, as best as anyone can tell, a pastor in eastern Tennessee preached that the Trinity was an abomination; that Jesus Christ alone was God. As such, the original name of the Church must be the Church of Jesus Christ. Any name appended before or after the name of Jesus Christ indicated a church of satan. This was, of course, derived from Revelation 17 wherein we read that the mother harlot (which would be Rome, if you are following along) had many daughters with many names. Suddenly, all of Protestantism was as evil as Luther's Catholic Church. This movement spread throughout the Appalachian area, from the mountains to the Appalachian diaspora in the mid-west where it met the rugged individualism of the new-rust belt. The one defining characteristic in this movement was the name on the building.

The Church of Jesus Christ is a movement of independent churches that rely heavily upon the King James, a subset of the King James Only movement, the pentecostal fire, the Nazarene idea of a second act of grace, and the fact that the name and only the name must be on the local church building. While not exclusionary at first, as time developed, The Church of Jesus Christ pulled out of fellowship with like-minded apostolic groups, or what the oneness pentecostals were often called. The best explanation I was given was that one day, someone read in a book that the Pope's residence was called the Apostolic Palace. Anything that remotely hinted at Catholicism was shunned. While not connected to the John Birch Society, many members held the same conspiratorial views. Thus, increasingly, the tiny communities grew deeper into isolation.

I was born in 1978, on warm January morning way down in Dixie. My mother was raised in a Southern Baptist home so she had some sense of a Christian foundation. Her partner in bringing me into this world was raised in a CEO family. That would be a Christmas and Easter Only family of church goers. At some point after I was born, he found religion when he and she and a group of friends decided to drunkenly enter into a little country church in Louisiana. After a spirit-filled environment that, from linguistic imagination, was little more than a bunch of drunks having a good time, feeding off one another.

I do not mean to disparage anyone; however, my parents were no doubt intoxicated with spirits while the church had imbibed what they believed to be the Spirit. A good word here may in fact be hysteria, as in mass — but not, and I mean *not*, Catholic mass.

So, they decide to return. And they, in the late seventies and the tip of the eighties, while the world watched the stand off between Iran and the United States awaiting the election of the fortieth president of this country, my life was changed by the miscalculation that certified Baptist drunks could change committed Spiritual drunkards.

My mother would leave my father shortly thereafter, my sister and I in tow. He was abusive, physically and emotionally. I can barely remember some of their fights. Mainly I remember the shouts that were different only in decibel level from the shouts at church and a cast-iron frying pan. Of course, the church took Shannon's side (that's the male part of the parental side) over Karen's (you guessed it; me mum). She wasn't saved. He was.

Saved? Well, she was raised in a Southern Baptist home and had given her profession of faith. But, this was not enough. To be "saved" in The Church of Jesus Christ you had to have repented, been baptized in the name of Jesus Christ, and then at some have received the gift of the Holy Ghost (not spirit, because that was Catholic) as evidenced by speaking in tongues (See Acts 2.38, but forget about Matthew 28.19 or 1st Corinthians 11). She had repented and I believe was baptized, but she had yet to speak in tongues, regardless of how many times they beat on her while she stood at the altar … Or how many times Shannon, because he wanted a ministry and to have a ministry one must have a saved wife … beat on her at home.

A divorce was appropriate at this time, I think, don't you? So that is what happened. A divorce. At some point, Shannon, thanks to the great State of Louisiana which could not see beyond the legal system and into the far future, was awarded joint custody. I was torn for a very long time between the strict — oh wait, I haven't explained that part yet.

The doctrines of The Church of Jesus Christ are pretty simple.

» Everything Catholic is evil (Rev 17.5-6).

» Protestants are Catholics; see above.

» The King James Bible was in fact good enough for Paul and Jesus; therefor it is good enough for me (Psalm 12.6-7). Also, the Catholics didn't use it.

» God generally hated you unless you were in his church (Lev 18.28; Rev 3.16).

» God had one church; it was not the Catholic Church. As a matter of fact, the Roman Catholic Church is the epitome of evil. And since they had the Apostolic Palace, all churches with the name Apostolic was Catholic too. I kid you not.

» The name of the Church must be only "The Church of Jesus Christ" (Eph 3.15).

» The pastor was absolute authority (Heb 13.17).

» Women were second class citizens (1 Co 14.34).

» Everyone was a sinner, even believers, so don't die because you really don't know if you will go to heaven (2 Thess 1.9).

» The body of a woman was evil. Women were not allowed to cut their hair (1 Co 11) or show anything that may be enticing to a man. Long skirts, even while swimming.

» The men got off pretty easy. Long pants, even while swimming. No long hair.

» No drinking, cussing, book reading (except the bible), and in Louisiana, no TV watching (Psalm 101.3). Unless they are hunting shows.

» Wives, listen to your husbands or else (Eph 5.22).[2]

There was a certain — how do you sinners say it? — legalistic attitude there? I remember when I was about seven years hearing

2 There are numerous websites for various local units, but this is one that seems to lay out the basic tenets: http://www.thechurchofjesuschrist-acts238.com/Beliefs.htm. See here as well: http://www.jesuschristisgod.org/Test%20Page%2010-27-09/Our%20Beliefs.htm. This one is interesting for the place it gives the KJV: http://www.tcjc-mi.org/whatwebelieve.html

a "prophecy" that someone, unsaved, was going to die that night. It was me; I knew it. I do not think I slept at all that night. This is not child abuse; this is raising up a child in the unadulterated fear of God.

I don't want you to think that it was all bad — there were people from my childhood, even in that little Greenwell Springs church house that I came to really love. For instance, and maybe the only one, Jean Etue. Wow, I haven't said that name for a while. She was the pastor's wife, a hardened women from the dust bowl of southern Arkansas. She had some rough patches about her — I'm a realist — but she loved me as a grandmother. I remember this one time, though, where she knew I was getting sick. She invited me to stay the night. I woke the next morning with a pretty serious fever.

Unbeknownst to her husband, the pastor, she took me to a pharmacy to get medicine. We, that church, believed only in faith healing. No medicine, no doctors, only faith. God rewarded you, or failed to reward you, based on your amount of faith. But, she took me and got some fever reducer.

It wasn't long before she died.[3] In 1995, late that year, she succumbed to what the faith healers thought was just "the change

---

3   I would like to tell you that she was the last death due to faith healing, but faith healing is still a practice in American churches as well as Christian churches across the world. See: "Couple Charged in Son's Faith Healing Death…", n.d. http://factnet.org/couple-charged-son-s-faith-healing-death.

"Death by Faith Healing: A Church-State Separation Dilemma", n.d. http://sojo.net/blogs/2012/04/18/death-faith-healing-church-state-separation-dilemma.

"Faith Healing Versus Traditional Medicine: Why Christians Don't Have to Choose." *theGrio*, n.d. http://thegrio.com/2012/09/04/faith-healing-versus-traditional-medicine-why-christians-dont-have-to-choose/.

Laing, Aislinn. "Cape Town Faith Healing Event Ends in One Death and 16 Injuries." *Telegraph.co.uk*, March 19, 2012, sec. worldnews. http://www.telegraph.co.uk/news/worldnews/africaandindianocean/southafrica/9154179/Cape-Town-faith-healing-event-ends-in-one-death-and-16-injuries.html.

of life" — what her daughter (also in the church) swore up and down was nothing more than a lack of faith. Real physicians called it cancer. For a year or more, she had suffered through a lot of pain. See, she couldn't go to the doctor, regardless of how bad she felt. I remember her tears and her halting steps, her haunting sighs. I remember the shouts of victory when the pastor would recount the story of how he was absolutely sure he was going to die when he passed a kidney stone years and years ago, so he was sure that she would overcome this demonic attack.

When they finally took her to the hospital, the doctors sent her home quickly. It wasn't about insurance, but because there was absolutely nothing they could do. She laid in the parsonage filled with morphine until she died. She suffered for many years, suffered until the last breath because she was afraid to break the rules; yet, for me, for just a fever, she snuck out and bought Tylenol.

Before the cancer, though, before that time, she was a sign of what to be. Yes, there were rough patches, but you could not find a better pastor's wife in our tradition.

Now, I need to separate something for you. You see, the church in Louisiana was connected to my later church in West Virginia. But, because the church organization which the West Virginia church was a part of was deemed too liberal, there were years of silence, of separation, of preaching in Baton Rouge against all others. See, our The Church of Jesus Christ was more saved than them — and thus, we should stay away from them. I'll get to the West Virginia experiences later, but I don't want you to think that they are lock-step with one another. Most of The Churches of Jesus

"New York City News - Breaking News in New York - NY Daily News." *New York Daily News*, n.d. http://articles.nydailynews.com/nydn-nav.php?c=17933673&p=NYDailyNews&t=ap-NY-DN9-G02&s=News&n=.

"Oregon Couple Convicted in Son's Faith-healing Death", n.d. http://latimesblogs.latimes.com/nationnow/2011/09/oregon-couple-convicted-in-sons-faith-healing-death.html.

Christ allow their members to go to the doctor for more than just the birth of children.

But, let me get back to my continued journey here.

My parents were by now divorced. Shannon went his way and my mother went hers. I followed Shannon of all people — dear God of all people. I, at least on the weekends I visited him, was the model member. Of course, as a boy, I didn't have much to shun, except women. That grew difficult later, as it always does, I guess.

When I was twelve, I made up my mind to transfer my domicile. I moved from my mother's custody to Shannon.

I refer to him by his first name because I need — deep down — to keep as much distance from him as possible. If I use the 'f' word in relation to Shannon, it is not father, I assure you.

He had promised me numerous things to move there, none of which were fulfilled. I would move out in three years, tired of Shannon more than I was of the Church. Of course, I wasn't saved. I had only repented of my sins and had been baptized twice — no three times — but had yet to speak in tongues. I shared earlier the night of dread. This is not the only fear I had.

In this church, the pastor had elevated a view on Revelation to a doctrinal level. Therefore, we lived with the constant threat that we were in the final day. FINAL DAY. We never knew when Jesus would return and destroy the wicked. And, according to the pastor, many of us were wicked and would be sent to hell with the worst Catholic sinner.

You would think that with this great preaching, the church would have grown, but would you believe that it did not?

Instead, it shrunk pretty fast. Before the major split, the Church numbered about a hundred. Nah, I'm joshing you. It numbered about ten. The pastor, the pastor's daughter and her family (5 in total), the pastor's son, a hold out, me and maybe Shannon. A major split occurred: Shannon left. Then the pastor's daughter and her family left. That's right — a congregation of ten couldn't get along.

The anger and legalistic self-entitling eschatology had influenced me. I did not care about anyone, really, because they were going to burn in hell. If someone did something to me at school, and I wasn't all that popular, I knew that God would get them sooner or later. If I liked a girl — and it was not me; I promise, I did not send those flowers with that note on Valentine's Day — then God had promised me a wife who he had established before the beginning of the world. See, the world was ours, and if the world mistreated us, they would get their comeuppance and we would get the reward, simply because we were the chosen very, very, very few. This anger grew in me, no doubt.

I moved back to my mother's when I was fifteen. My mother by then was divorced from her second or third husband (I think she was married in between Shannon and her last husband, but I'm not sure). She was quite simply an alcoholic. Because her life was a mess, my grandfather took us in. Not liking the idea that she couldn't drink herself into oblivion each and every note, she and my sister left to go back to Louisiana. I stayed. This was July of 1994. For a year — and I sometimes, when life is especially difficult I go back to our house in Mississippi, if even in my mind — I lived with my grandfather and forgot how to wear a watch. I explored what it meant to be free of hate, anger, and to know only the love God. But, he died in June of 1995. I wish I could tell you more about him, about how he influenced my life, how his peace of Christ came back to me later in life to comfort me, but that is a bit difficult at the moment.

After the funeral, I moved back to my mothers until I could not handle the drinking. I started to go back to The Church of Jesus Christ where I was infused again with the entitled eschatology, leading to anger, leading to the desire to control everyone else. I moved from my mother's house to Shannon's mother to whom I as a seventeen year old had to pay rent. My mother promised to help me get a car with the money she inherited.

I remember this evening well. Today is Wednesday, it was a September evening in south Louisiana. I am outside, oh the phone when my mother tells me she will not get me a car.

I have inherited Shannon's temper. I am white-faced with anger. I am trembling. I think about my words carefully. I parse my words carefully. I tell her, "I hate you and I never want to see you again. If I come to your funeral, it will be a cold day in hell."

That Saturday, I was sitting on the back row in the church house. The preacher whose name I cannot spell was preaching a sermon I cannot remember. I remember thinking that if my mother heard this, she would come to her senses and maybe even get back in this Church. I didn't want my mother going to hell, for the most part. We were taught that it was okay to be okay with some people going to hell — Catholics and Protestants for instance. I didn't want my mother going, however. So I wrote down the verses and some thoughts. I decided to call her on Monday, to tell her how sinful she was. I was, of course, perfect. I had judged her and found her guilty.

Jean Etue, as I mentioned above, was struggling with pain so she decided to say home that night. Home was the parsonage built on to the back of the church. She came into the back of the church, smiled, and motioned for her son to come out. She came back in and I turned to my friend and laughed about who was in trouble now. This happened again.

The second time, he came in and pulled both me and my friend out with him. Once outside, she told me that at about 2pm that afternoon, my mother had died in a car accident. So many thoughts — including my regret at never having gotten to tell her how sorry I was.

For her not believing in The Church of Jesus Christ and thus, ending up in hell that every night.

Later, to be sure, I have come to regret my final words to her — to regret my anger, my superiority, my view of a woman, even my mother, as a second class citizen. But those were the last words I said to my mother.

Sometimes, I wonder if I insist on a belief in the afterlife to make sure I have the chance to apologize.

All of this is part of my story – it is not just the bad doctrine, but the fruits of the doctrine. That is why I have started at the beginning and I am walking you through my life story. There is no real separation between the doctrines and teachings I received and my life story. They infected me. They plagued me. They plague me still. You — I want the readers the understand just how entrenched these doctrines were in my psyche.

Fundamentalism is about control. It is not about legalism, nor bad doctrine — no these things are the tools used or the programs that naturally develop from the control that is sought. The pastor is the absolute authority over the church, and as a church member, over you and me. The husband has the absolute control over the wife and family. If there is a kink in the chain, then you will lose acceptance. Therefore, you, if you seek acceptance — i.e., the assuredness you are going to heaven — will do what you have to do. That motivation to acceptance takes many forms, but it is related all back to the idea of control. You control, or perhaps you seek to control, because you are controlled. It is very much like the clichè of a bully we know from the movies. Because the bully is bullied at home, he will bully where he can to regain some sense of control.

I would wager that the lack of control that drives fundamentalists is the changing nature of the world. In the early part of the twentieth century, when the fundamentalists first emerged, they were were led by intellectuals from Princeton who desired to retain some of the basic biblical tenets in light of the German-led historical criticism that had finally reached the American shores.[4] These early intellectuals were varied in several ways, but all retained five

---

4   Barr, James. *Fundamentalism.* 2nd Revised ed. SCM Press, 2010.
"Christian Fundamentalism." Wikipedia, the Free Encyclopedia, November 8, 2012. http://en.wikipedia.org/w/index.php?title=Christian_fundamentalism&oldid=520567960.
Marsden, George M. *Fundamentalism and American Culture.* 2nd ed. Oxford University Press, USA, 2006.

key points, including miracles, the Virgin Birth, and the inerrancy of Scripture. When fundamentalism reached the more rural areas of American Christianity, it was used as a preventive measure against change. This all happened as the world was opened up due to the once Great War. As Americans retuned in droves from Europe with new ideas, the new movement, instead of setting down boundaries, became geared to exclusion and eventually to isolation. In 1925, fundamentalism engaged the American legal system and lost.[5] It went into hiding.

The world was changing, and to be honest, so was Christianity; yet, instead of engaging the secular world and the changes it was making in Christianity, fundamentalism plugged its ears, turned its head, and denied that it was in fact the twentieth century. They sought to control the role the world played in the church and so they began to control their members. New, stricter, sects emerged — my former one is one of them. Women were now the root of all evil. Public Education was a bane. The King James Version was and is the only bible around; after all, if it was good enough for Jesus and Paul, then by good God above, it is good enough for me.

When the Christian world began to heal itself, sects like mine moved further away, in the opposite direction, recovering some of the worst parts of the Reformers' anti-Catholic doctrines. My argument here is this: fundamentalism is about control. Therefore, it has

---

Marsden, Mr George. *Reforming Fundamentalism: Fuller Seminary and the New Evangelicalism.* Wm. B. Eerdmans Publishing Company, 1995.
Ruthven, Malise. *Fundamentalism: A Very Short Introduction.* Oxford University Press, 2007.
Torrey, R. A. Dixon, A. C. , et al (editors). *The Fundamentals.* Baker Book House, Grand Rapids, MI, U.S.A., 2008.
5   Mencken, H. L. *A Religious Orgy in Tennessee: A Reporter's Account of the Scopes Monkey Trial.* Melville House, 2006.
Larson, Edward J. *Summer for the Gods: The Scopes Trial and America's Continuing Debate Over Science and Religion.* First Trade Paper ed. Basic Books, 2006.
Moran, Jeffrey P. *The Scopes Trial: A Brief History with Documents.* Bedford/St. Martin's, 2002.

created doctrines one must accept to be accepted; clothing styles one must wear to be accepted; attitudes, postures, thoughts that lead to acceptance. And where something could control them, they dismiss it. Tradition is the worst enemy of the fundamentalist. The accountability the ecumenical spirit lays down must be challenged. Science and advancements in thought are of the devil.

CONTROL

Once my mother died, it was not long before I lost Jean Etue. I graduated high school at some point. I wasn't an overall terrible young man, but I wasn't perfect either. I would like to think that what kept me from myself during these years was what Wesleyans call the Grace that Goes Before — that constant hand of God upon the person, preparing them for the actual call of God to come to repentance. I am sure, however, that is trips to the altar to offer two minutes worth of prayer and forty minutes thinking about Star Trek.

That was a huge fear of mine growing up — that God would come back before the next Star Trek movie was released. Sure, most of us would have been happy had God somehow stopped the fifth movie, but he didn't.

I went to college against the wishes of near about everyone. After a few years, I met someone there that was my first love, but like all first loves, it was a disaster. See, we weren't allowed to date. I didn't date until I was 19 and out of the house. This was a pretty stiff rule that we have to follow. I remember one time, when I was 15, Shannon caught a small smile shared between a girl and I as we walked past each other. He had picked me up from a weekend at my mother's, I think, and it just happened. I was smacked around a few times that night.

I was never really physically abused — don't get me wrong. There was the time just mentioned and a time when I informed Shannon that at 18 I would move it. I was 13 at the time, I believe? We were riding on the road and no sooner had the words come out of my mouth then did he have a hand of my hair and was throwing me around the cab of the truck until I said that I would not move out until he told me I could. It wasn't that he didn't want to be more physically abusive, I'm sure, but I was a boy. Abuse was for women.

Let me back up and fill in a gap. Remember when I said that at one time my church in Baton Rouge had associated with other churches, particularly one in West Virginia? When I was about six or so, Shannon came to West Virginia on a revival or something like that. A man in the church here decided that he needed to marry off his daughters in a hurry because of sin of the world. The oldest refused to marry Shannon, but it wasn't really her choice. See, she had a child already and therefore was not prize material, if you know what I mean. The man's sixteen year old daughter was the one chosen to marry the 27 year old man after only a few days. Within a few months, she had moved down to Louisiana to be a child bridge.

This woman — this teenage girl who had never been out of the hollow — had to have been the most beautiful girl I had ever seen. She was also so tremendously happy, fearless, and ready to be the wife the Bible told her to be. She and Shannon were together for about two years, I think, before she absconded with my youngest sister back to West Virginia. I had head that on a return trip she had cheated on him and decided to stay at home. This was not the case. No, this was not the case at all.

So, back to the story. Eventually, I would meet my wife. We had a child. I was out of church, of course. Because, well, she wasn't my wife. This was a scary time you see. When my wife was pregnant with my daughter, we awoke one morning to the feeling that in short order, our life was about to change. My daughter was on her way. We showed up at the hospital, went through the processes in record time and suddenly, we were in the cold delivery room. Three times now I've been in a delivery room, but that was the coldest.

"Push!" the nurses yelled.

And suddenly, my daughter stopped, a sure sign of how obstinate she would become in her pre-teen years. She had changed her mind, obviously, and no amount of talking would convince her to move. The medical staff were getting worried. Her heart rate was down. It was looking serious. You all know what could happen if a baby stays in the birth canal for too long and some of you know what may cause the baby's heart rate to suddenly drop. So, they called for the forceps.

In the tradition I was raised in, I was a sinner who, while once saved and all that, was "out of church" so I had two choices — repent or wait for hell to swallow me up. God would only hear that repenting prayer, but nothing else and if that. Regardless, I began to pray. I had heard too much about forceps and babies and the injuries that could happen — and this was before the days of Dr. Google. But this was getting serious. So, I prayed, silently while sitting at my wife's head, both of us nervous — the room colder, darker, quieter...

In a flash, just a second or two, — I can still remember every position, ever color, every smell that happened in those long hours that were nothing but minutes before the doctor came in with the bright shiney forceps.

I was worried. But I prayed. It wasn't a particularly insightful prayer. Nor a loud one. Pretty sure it was all of five words.

But at the exact moment as those words drew to a close — at the exact moment when the doctor walked in with those man-eating claws, my daughter was born.

When she was cleaned up and we finally got to hold her, there was this little finger tip size red splotch on her eyelid. To me, this looked like where someone — something – had touched her. This was and is still today something that even as I seek to explain so very much, remains beyond my reach.

I am telling you this because I want you to understand the many chances I had to leave fundamentalism, but chose rather to stay.

Shortly after my first daughter was born, my then-girlfriend and I decided to get married. I was still in contact with the former-pastor's daughter who was now a pastor's wife because, as

I said, earlier, they had split. Her words were pretty simple. We would love to marry you, but first, she said, you have to join the church and pay tithes. We would later marry in a Baptist Church. Don't look at me like that. Yes, I know what that sounds like. I was living in sin, but I had to pay to get out of it. This was not the only oddity this woman produced. She proudly boasted that she had kept someone from joining the church until the young soul had voided her life of all sin. See, you had to be sinless before you could repent.

In 1996, I came to West Virginia for the first time. I loved it. Immediately. I wanted to move there since that first dawn. In October of 2002, with an unexpected wife and child in tow, I moved to Miami, West Virginia.

We moved to where my former stepmother was. I had reconnected with her a few years ago and she gave us our first home (rented) in West Virginia. Remember that beautiful woman I told you about — the woman that had caused a six year old boy to go flush at the sight of her, to run and cower of embarrassment? When I met her again, she had been married several more times, had several more children, drank lot, smoked, was beat up by the world and others, and hated. She hated. She hated that she hated and so that made her hate some more. She was not the same person I once knew. Come to find out — no, let me cut this out of the story and just say she was physically in many ways abused, emotionally in many ways abused, and spiritually in many ways abused. No, not since she left Shannon, as if God was punishing her for that, but by Shannon and under the authority of The Church of Jesus Christ.

When we moved to West Virginia, I was not a good person. I was selfish, angry, and my mouth was as vulgar as, well, I don't know, but it was vulgar. I hadn't hit my wife, but I used the power of the tongue to belittle her as much as possible. She wised up. She decided to move out. She called her mom and brother and they were on their way to get her, up from Louisiana. In the space of twenty-four hours, I emptied everything out to God, begging him not to let my family move. I promised everything, including that

I would attend church again. See, we were about 3 miles from the Church of Jesus Christ at Ohley. Of course we were always taught that they were just this side of too far gone, but I bargained and pleaded with God.

My wife decided to stay.

I'm not going to lie. I changed. I changed for the better. I didn't curse. I controlled my temper better. I attempted to live the life I was supposed to live. The following Sunday, I went to the church service at Ohley. I was welcomed with open arms and why shouldn't I be? We were the perfect demographic for a church — the growing family. My wife didn't believe. In God. She didn't believe in God. Her family was Baptist, but they were horrible people as well. So, why would she believe anything? Anyway, at a revival service she came to believe, repented of her sins in a grand and glorious display of the out pouring of the spirit and in the middle of a cold winter, was baptized in running water.

Don't get me wrong. The changes experienced by both my wife and myself were real. This was the first time I had felt like the Church of Jesus Christ was real. We could watch TV, go to the doctor, and there wasn't a lot of hate. At first. There was an organization, which meant more people going to heaven. Not just us four and no more. It was a new day for me and my faith. I cannot and will not discount those experiences either of the Spirit or of the awakening, love, and fellowship. My wife can hardly discount the good things either.

But, in our time there, we noticed an anger issue with the pastor, favoritism for a select few including ourselves, and some other double talk. During this time, my wife was being beat at the altar. Not to the altar, but at the altar. Not at home, but at Church. This is the way you get the Holy Ghost, you know — having someone beat it into you. At least one time, she wanted to quit Church — at least one time she told me about.

I couldn't let her. I was selfish. I listened to her complaints about not liking anyone there anymore; about not feeling anything anymore. But I insisted she kept going. There is a reason for this.

I was not particularly worried about her soul, but I was worried about preaching. Oh. I missed that part. Yeah, once I got there, as a young man who was educated and knew how to talk/read, I was passively drafted into the ministry. I say passively because Brenda would drop hints to my wife about the pastor seeing something special in me. Things like that. So, I announced that I was going to preach. Amen. Glory.

But see, to preach your wife had to be in order. She had to be obedient. She had to be there. So, even if she was sick, I made sure my wife attended so that I could preach. This was something along the same lines the church in Louisiana had practiced, which gave license for Shannon to beat his second wife. Either she was there, or else. This was an attempt at molding as well. See, I was being groomed for the next-to-the pastor spot. I have no need to brag when I tell you this, but I was by far the best minister at that church. Trust me when I say this.

But my pigheadedness got in the way. I questioned things, demanded that things be consistent. That didn't go over too well. Within a year, we had decided to leave The Church of Jesus Christ at Ohley and go to the one in Montgomery. I was allowed to stay there until I felt like it was time to go back. I went back after four months or so. Again, things weren't right. Things weren't honest. We left. We came back.

This time, it stuck, I think. This time we had every intention of staying no matter what, and indeed, we turned our backs on some of the internal problems we were facing. I became a minister again. And you know what? This time it was good. I mean really good. I loved it. Don't get me wrong. I believe the Spirit works and we can experience it. Granted, now I am more apt to experience it reading a book or standing on the verge of finding a solution to some problem than I am preaching. But then, I was the little red-headed Cajun preacher. I was a bible thumper. I was good.

But, I was on the way to Damascus when my eyes were opened. I couldn't watch the disparity any longer. I think what finally broke me here was watching someone stand up in Church, lie about the pastor and pronounce his impending marriage. The pastor had previous counseled against the marriage, but the young man in question decided he wanted to be married after knowing his soon-to-be-wife for just a few weeks. You would think that with protections afforded Traditional Marriage, the pastor, especially after he was thrown into the mix unwillingly, would have said no. But, he did not. When it came time for the wedding, which occurred after a Sunday evening service, my wife and I left. During that time, I decided that I was to stay in the church, for better or worse, I had to devoid myself of any responsibility.

See, I believe that with authority comes responsibility. As a minister, I was only allowed to preach. But, what could I preach about if I could not speak about the problems surrounding us? Instead, I was told that I could only preaching "evangelistic" messages — I was preaching about the need of repentance to those who had been in the same pew for 20 years. I broke with that, and no one seemed to mind. But I couldn't preach any longer with integrity if I could not preach what needed to be preached. So, one Sunday after the morning service, I told the pastor I was stepping away from the ministry. He asked why and I told him I wouldn't tell him. Come to find out, he knew all along that I disagreed with him about letting all sorts of problems fester.

I began to work with a pastor in Michigan on building a documentary on the Trinity. We were not Trinitarians. But, the world needed to know why it was evil and where it came from. We had timed the recording of this to coincide with the usual May tent revival.

I want to step back again to remind you that it was not all bad times. By the time my son was born, we were settled into the Church of Jesus Christ at Ohley and had become pretty close with Paul and Brenda, the Pastor and his wife. So much so that when my son was born, we had asked her to be in the delivery room and we named my son, the middle name, after the pastor. We were close. He would share real stuff with me, not just gossip. I would help him out and he would help me out. I was, as I said, being groomed and I was enjoying the part. I considered Paul a friend, a mentor, and a beloved pastor. I could not understand how anyone could say anything bad about him. Even when I had doctrinal issues with the Presiding Bishop Spence he defended me and even preached against Spence at least one time.

He also encouraged me to pursue reading, to pursue theology, to read other bible translations, to use the Apocrypha. To be okay with a less than plain sense reading. I remember the conversation where I asked him about using the Apocrypha. See, these books, while in the KJV originally and a particular favorite of closeted-Catholic King James, were thrown out by later publishers as Protestantism in the United States became more Protestant. Luther had challenged them — but then again, he didn't like Revelation (couldn't understand it), James (understood it too well), and Hebrews (suggested that Luther may in fact be hell bound). So Protestants had placed them in the index or between the testaments. I discovered that the Wisdom of Solomon has something to say about the Gospels. So, I asked him if it was okay to read these books, and use them. He was okay with that. He was not as deep seated fundamentalist at that point. He was even more liberal than me on Genesis 1. When it came to the King James issue I had read a book about the history of the English Bible.[6] It began to turn my affections away from the King James Version. Granted I moved towards the Tyndale version, but still, I began to discover other translations. Paul was even okay with this. Thus, I posted on my blog and other public places verses from other translations as well as used these other versions in blog posts.

Back to the Tent Revival …

The Tent Revival started on Saturday with the men of the church showing up to set up the recovered circus tent. I noticed that I was given a cool reception. Maybe it was just because it was May and the early morning air …. No not even worth making an excuse. See, I had caused a fuss about the Church news paper. A

6   Daniell, David. *The Bible in English: Its History and Influence.* Yale University Press, 2003.

minister from The Church of Jesus Christ in Portage, Indiana had written an article in the Church organ that declared that the Bible is just like Jesus, but on paper. I responded but it never got published. Of course, I responded and it was read, but it never got published.[7] No doubt, I had angered a few people. Plus, I was railing against the idea that it was the Father who had died on the Cross. This made no sense and would create a theological paradox, regardless of what Pope St. Zephyrinus had to say.[8] As oneness believers, we believed that Jesus was his own father. So some of this may in fact be the reason why I received a cool reception.

Come to find out, the Bishop from Tennessee and the presiding Bishop went to my pastor, also a bishop, to discuss my heretical actions. I was to be brought into obedience. On Thursday evening, during the altar call of the Tent Revival, my pastor — the same one who had encouraged me to use other translations — approached me to tell me that the other bishops and some of their members had questioned me. You know, being saved and all. His only response about the KJV issue was to simply say that he only preached from the KJV. I remember feeling pretty darn abandoned at that point. He was pretty timid about the entire thing. I canceled the presentation and set about deciding what I needed to do. I was let down and I was hurt.

After the tent revival was over, I remember posting a verse on Facebook from the NIV. Funny story. I guess my pastor's daughter-in-law (who by the way, escaped that nonsense; I hold nothing against her) had seen it who then reported it to the pastor's wife who promptly started to yell, scream, and shout at the pastor about the evils I had brought upon the(m) Church. It got so bad, he said,

---

7 Watts, Joel L. "Is the Bible the Word of God? No." *Unsettled Christianity*, n.d. http://unsettledchristianity.com/2008/12/is-the-bible-the-word-of-god-no/.

8 Kirsch, J.P. (1912). "Pope St. Zephyrinus." In The Catholic Encyclopedia. New York: Robert Appleton Company. Retrieved November 10, 2012 from New Advent: http://www.newadvent.org/cathen/15756c.htm.

that he had to leave the house to call me to ask me to just tone it down a bit. I didn't refuse, but I said I would give it some time.

I did. In about a week or so, I posted again. Here's the thing – I was not posting out of spite, but because I was trying to appeal to a broad audience. I mean, if you read Philippians 2 in the NLT (1st Edition) it is much clearer than the KJV at this point. But, this raised the ire of the malcontents in other churches. I was roundly attacked, on Facebook, but my brothers and sisters in Christ. It got pretty heated. I mean, how dare I post a bible verse on Facebook! Well, it wasn't a bible verse, I guess, since it was NIV. Whew …

I received a call from the pastor who was on his way out of town. He didn't tell me why, but he was pretty upset emotionally, but not angry. He said that he had some family issues to work out but that he would tell me everything later. But, he asked if I could not post anything for a while, on Facebook or on the blog. I agreed.

I had sensed something was going on, and I got bits and pieces until after it was said and done. The pastor met me at the McDonald's one morning to tell me the story. Now, I do not want you to think me callous or ready to tell this story, but it is needed. I had been abused. My mother had been abused. My former stepmother had been abused. My wife had been abused. All by, in, and because of The Church of Jesus Christ. But, what happened here is even now something that cannot compare.

There are legal issues here that are best not explored, as it may take away from the thrust of this story. So, I have muted much, changed names here, but the truth is the same. Mark was a young man of twelve years old when he began to be molested. See, Mark was a gifted and talented person with a soul of the muses. He did not hunt or fish or do anything else young boys were expected to do at his age. Unfortunately, he fell prey to a predator and as we have seen too often on the news and in the headlines, our friend was robbed of certain innocence.

After a time where our friend stood up for himself, he witnessed the predator moving on to other prey. Our friend had had enough. In what amounts to one of the greatest acts of courage

I've seen, he divulged everything to his grandparents after that summer camp (the year before the tent revival). He divulged that he thought he was gay and even had a boyfriend. There is no doubt that you and I would praise this young man for his courage and his awareness. Further, you and I would think something would have been done then, but it was not. Well, something happened. Mark's family emotionally abused him.[9]

Mark told his grandparents in early October. They waited a month before they told the parents of the newest prey. Come to find out, the younger man's parents had suspected something after finding illicit text messages between the two. The predator was also fond of sleeping over and making the prey close his door.

Over the holidays, prayers went up, but that was about it. No one said anything about the predator. No one reported him to the police. It was decided the two preys would be kept away from the predator.

After the tent revival, a northern addressed concerns that our friend didn't look the part and was exhibiting some gayness. Seriously, that was the charges. The Portage church wanted him to stop playing the piano.

It came to a head when the presiding officers (called Bishops) met. For the time being, the predator and the prey would have to step off the platform (no playing music in church). There was a huge blow up, with threats made and the like. No police were involved. Only prayers and time off for bad behavior. Behaviors were hid, actions muted. No one reported anything to the official authorities. Of course, only the presiding officers and the parents of the boys in question knew what was happening.

I remember asking our pastor if our friend would get counseling. He said that he believed that since they had prayed about it, he would be okay. Our friend had prayed really, really good and you know, that's all that matters. The younger man, the second prey, would not get counseling either but would remain in the

9 "What Are You? A Fag?" *Unsettled Christianity*, n.d. http://unsettled-christianity.com/2009/09/what-are-you-a-fag/.

same church as the pedophile who had as his sole punishment the inability to play piano for the church. Eventually, the Dyersburg church left or was kicked out, with some of the members deciding to stay with the organization.

I also asked our pastor if the police were going to be called. He said no. I reminded him of what the law requires, both in Tennessee and in West Virginia. He still said no. He was confident that nothing else needed to happen. He asked if either my wife or I had anything against our friend. That statement still strikes me as odd. But he did say something to me, as we were walking out of the joint, that chills me to this very day. He looked at me and said that he fully suspected that other boys had been molested by the predator, but that it would have to be up to their parents to determine it and then decide if *they* wanted to call the cops.

No police as of today, to my knowledge, have been called. I did call CPS, but nothing happened. Because no official charges were filed … stories like this in print become a legal issue for the one telling them.

One church split from the organization over the punishment of the predator and not the punishment of the prey. Of course, over the next few months, various factions in that church split as well.

The other church split once or twice as well.

In a related incident, a church in Michigan split away from the main organization because the pastor could finally take no longer the amount of lies the chief presiding officer told as presiding bishop.

Granted, many of these little sects have banded together at one time or the other for or against one another. Instead of looking at the real problem, they would rather blame others for the bad fruit. Oh well.

So, how did I finally leave?

One night on Facebook, before I met with the pastor, I engaged a young man from one church who told me a lot of the stuff that was going on — except the molestation stuff. Come to find out, the youth group there did not believe the molestation charges against the predator, believing him to be innocent. According to this young man, everyone knew our friend was gay. That's why they were angry. Our friend still played the piano but the predator was not allowed too. The conservation was recorded via the chat feature on Facebook.

It was then sent to the northern pastor and then to our pastor among others in the organization. This move saved me.

I received a call about midnight that evening of the meeting at McDonald's. He was reading the conversation that had been circulated. I could hear voices in the background raising a pretty serious fuss. A bad fuss. I was now the one completely at fault for everything. This had happened before, threatened me, and ridiculed the lot of us. But this time was different. How dare I let it out of the bag that something was simply not right. I could hear some pretty awful things coming my way. I knew they were hurt, but to honestly not do anything except to the person who dared question everything? Really?

At that moment, when I got off the phone, my wife and I decided we would never go back. We were done.[10] I was done.[11] There was no real decision made. We would never go back.

---

10 Watts, Joel L. "To My Brothers and Sisters in Portage TCOJC (B)." *Unsettled Christianity*, n.d. http://unsettledchristianity.com/2009/10/to-my-brothers-and-sisters-in-portage-tcojc-b/.

———. "Why I Left Church." *Unsettled Christianity*, n.d. http://unsettledchristianity.com/2009/12/why-i-left-church/.

11 For the full view-meltdown, see : Watts, Joel L. "Portage." *Unsettled Christianity*, n.d. http://unsettledchristianity.com/tag/portage/. While writing this chapter, I was faced with the possibility that such statements — the charges that crimes had been committed for instance — could not be sustained. I would offer three points. First, I have emails that plainly state that the pastors of the Church organization knew and purposely hide the child molestation. Second, I have a pretty wide internet trial (For instance, "Why I Left Church." *Unsettled Christianity*, n.d. http://unsettledchristianity.com/2009/12/why-i-left-church/.) Third, I made a report to CPS in WV who was unable to do anything because no one would testify to it.

During the September after my defection, I was confronted by a pastor, a friend, from Michigan about my disobedience to the pastor at Ohley. I remember it well. He suggested that the one time he saw me not buckle up my children was the exact same thing as the pastor not reporting child molestation.[12] Imagine that, for a moment. Because you had a really crowded car, namely because I was carrying the Michigan pastor around, I could not fully buckle up my child, I could say nothing about letting a serial pedophile go loose. The main reason for not reporting the child molestation, it seems, was because of how bad it would look on The Church of Jesus Christ. I kid you not. Lives were destroyed, with the good possibility that more would be destroyed and all we were worried about was the image of the Church and being obedient to the pastor. Wow.

Certainty, like control, is another hallmark of fundamentalism. They go and in hand, come to think of it. Let us define certainty as the ability to do mental gymnastics to hide facts. For instance, young earth creationism. Regardless of facts produced from Church Tradition, from contemporary myths by other Ancient Near Eastern cultures, and finally from science those like Ken Ham and others who believe in a young earth will discover new and powerful ways to deny all sorts of evidence.[13] The reasoning mind of the Fundamentalist is molested to believe only what they can plainly read in Scripture. While this creates a hermeneutical spiral and is simply illogical, what matters most is that the person with the

12 Watts, Joel L. "Question to My Readers – Child Molestation and Seat Belt Laws." *Unsettled Christianity*, n.d. http://unsettledchristianity. com/2009/09/question-to-my-readers-child-molestation-and-seat-belt-laws/.

13 Walton, John. *Ancient Near Eastern Thought and the Old Testament: Introducing the Conceptual World of the Hebrew Bible.* Baker Academic, 2006.

Walton, John H. Genesis 1 as Ancient Cosmology. Eisenbrauns, 2011.

———. The Lost World of Genesis One: Ancient Cosmology and the Origins Debate. IVP Academic, 2009.

Bible in his or her hands is the final arbiter of what Scripture really means.[14] We come to believe in a black and white world where it is an either or. Either The Church of Jesus Christ is completely true or it is completely false. Granted, this seems a tad bit quaint; however, this is the same methodology applied by other sects to Christianity as a whole. They, these sects assume, are completely wrong. Sure, other words may be said, but if, say, Methodism, has the same faults as independent Baptists, why aren't we all Methodists? Certainty helps us to control the influx of facts and information. Anything that challenges our previous beliefs is automatically wrong.

Thus, imagine when you are pretty certain that the white in your black and white world is black and your black is white. The mental damage caused by such a radical change in mental situation can kill the Christian. There are no real good analogies I can think of, but if you've heard of amputees, this one might help. An amputee who has suddenly lost his or her legs can still feel them, can still at times without thought take a step to go for a walk. When the wind blows, the legs hurt. But the legs aren't there. There is nothing there. Yet, the mind is still convinced the appendages remain, can feel them, and can still control them.

Now, imagine the amputee with legs unexpectantly torn off in a battle or a car accident. This amputee, instead of seeking medical care, decides that he, that I, can simply ignore the pain, the blood, the gore. He finds some sticks and manufacturers his own prosthetics. He uses a needle and thread to sew up the wounds. What would you then expect to happen? If he didn't bleed out (many in transition do), he would get gangrene and the wound would begin to stink, to fester, to pus. He would suddenly see the prosthetics for what they are, dead tree limbs. In the middle of going to work one day, the pain and the false pride that prevented him from seeking medical care would come crashing down. He has a choice. He can either lie down and die or seek help.

---

14 Osborne, Grant R. *The Hermeneutical Spiral: A Comprehensive Introduction to Biblical Interpretation*. Revised and Expanded. IVP Academic, 2006.

My journey with The Church of Jesus Christ was over and done with, or so I thought. As much trouble has I had had with this group over the years, as much anger and hate it had produced, as much abuse I had seen done in its name one would think that leaving the group after this molestation situation would have been easy.

It was and then it wasn't. We left in late June 2009. However, we maintained our clothing, our appearance, our way of life. On Sunday mornings, we would gather around the table and have a devotional while reading the bible.[15] We followed the church calendar and on the first Sunday of the month, we would celebrate communion with real wine. At times, my wife would lead it; my daughter too. It was fine.

I pictured myself as David who waited in Philistia until Saul was dead. I just knew God wanted me to go and save The Church of Jesus Christ and get it back on track. I still believed in the basic tenets of The Church of Jesus Christ. We alone were right. We alone had the proper doctrine. We alone had the truth.

Therefore, I intended to stay and wait out justice. Surely, Justice would arrive, the pedophile would be in jail. I was concerned with the goings on at the place in Ohley, although I had been plainly, by now, excommunicated. I was not allowed to go back to the place in Ohley and we were off limits to everyone. We were banned, shunned, and exiled. But I knew that one day ... one day ... God would bring me back and everything would be okay.

That never happened.

Instead, I was alone. With my wife and children, alone.

We celebrated Advent, sort of, and then went full bore into Lent. During this time, the tragedy at Upper Big Branch occurred and due to my day job, I was heavily involved in the follow-up investigation. I was there, that night, waiting.[16] When a tragedy

---

15 Credo, ed. *Holy Bible: Mosaic NLT*. Tyndale House Publishers, Inc., 2009.

16 Watts, Joel L. "25 Miners, 25 Men, 25 Families – And Counting." *Unsettled Christianity*, n.d. http://unsettledchristianity.com/2010/04/25-

strikes like this, you need a support system. I did not have it. Suddenly, my illusionary world of God's justice came crashing down. Those at fault for Upper Big Branch would not be brought to justice; those who had allowed a young man to rape at least two young boys and not to mention the pedophile himself, would not be brought to justice. Suddenly, God was gone.

All of this was building up in me. The anger at God, the frustration. The abandonment. The growing finality of never going back to The Church of Jesus Christ. All of this was like a storm that waits just off shore until no one believes it will strike. Then, suddenly, it did.

On a Saturday afternoon, my wife and I couldn't handle it. We blew up at each other over something that no longer matters. I was pretty sure she was hiding something from me. She was. I finally got it out of her. She said that she was tired of living "this way." She didn't like the dresses, she wanted to cut her hair, she wanted our daughter to no longer be the odd duck in school.

My immediate response was the promise of a divorce and a bold statement that I was done waiting. I was going back to The Church of Jesus Christ with or without her.

Done.

But that was instinct. That was fear. I had just lost control of the situation.

She went on to say she was done with God and religion that it had brought her nothing by grief.

These words were the words that had struck me hard. These were the words that suddenly brought everything I had managed to bottle up out.

My grandfather was a deacon in the Southern Baptist Church. His Christian walk was difficult. He and my grandmother had adopted two children that, well, tested them in all things. Through the struggles of trying to re-raise my mother and then, for a year, raise me, he had taught me so very much about the fruits of the spirit. He showed me love, joy, peace, patience, temperance. He showed

---

miners-25-men-25-families-and-counting/.

me the image of God. It took me so very long to see it without looking at it through the lens of my fundamentalistic expectations.

One of his sisters, Norma Nail, is a great aunt of mine and she shared with me that she relied often on Psalm 139 to help her through. This had long since been my strength as well. She too showed me the fruits of the spirit. She loves those who had hurt her, was patient, was kind, was joyful, and even as she was losing her eye sight and independence, peaceful. My two aunts, May and Nornie, have been a guiding force in so many ways that the words here cannot express, and great in every sense of the word. They were always non-judgmental, loving, Christian — but guiding with soft rebukes and helpfulness I cannot share. Both have shown me the happiness a Christian can enjoy *as a Christian.*

A dear friend of ours, Ellen, another Baptist, had herself experienced too much to still be kind. But she was. Her heart is as big as God's I think. These three people, and a few more, rushed to my mind during those seconds of silence.

See, I realized at that moment what the fruits of the Spirit really were. It was not telling everyone they were hell bound while being jealous of their liberty. Indeed, The Church of Jesus Christ exemplifies well the works of the flesh. We encourage fornication because teach only abstinence. Thus, when our children would "sin out" they would more often than not engage in premartial sex, become pregnant, and return to church to be shamed.[17] We are impure, filled with hate. There are no days in The Church of Jesus Christ not filled with envy, jealousy, strife (for example, there are something like twenty different The Churches of Jesus Christ in Dyersburg, all coming from the first one). We love our quarrels, our dissensions, our factions, our enmities. We murder one another with our words; we fail to protect the innocent, the children, the lowly. We have made the King James Version our idol. We have made our interpretation, our idol. We have made God an idol.

---

17 "U.S. Teen Birthrates Are Down, But Still High in These States", n.d. http://www.theatlanticcities.com/politics/2012/04/teen-birthrates-are-way-down-still-high-these-states/1735/.

But, when I looked at those who were hell bound sinners because they were not us, I could find only the fruits of the spirit. I found love, joy, peace, gentleness, and self-control. Peace, dear God, I found peace. It was there, in the eyes of my aunts, of my friends, of those who had more faith than fear.

In those few seconds the truth of the matter came rushing in.

For a while, I had denied the progression of my theological leanings.

I was deep into studying Scripture from an academic standpoint. I had entered what we affectionately call the biblioblogosphere where I had engaged scholars, read different bible translations, began to grasp real philosophy and real theology, and most of all, was encouraged to faithfully think through the sacred tradition I had been given. I would often joke that the most dangerous thing to give a fundamentalist is a book, but I think it is more than this. I think that within each of us, if we are not afraid to show it, is an inherent ability to question and to reason. Fundamentalism suppresses this basic human trait. Scripture tells that where the Spirit is, there is Liberty, there is a boldness of speech. Yet, in fundamentalism, even in the most spirited of churches, the mind is placed in a dungeon, told daily that there are monsters outside. The mind, like all unused muscles, atrophies. It is like a sort of neuro-myopathy. We are given reason, logic, compassion — passion — senses, an neurons by the Creator and yet fundamentalism denies us the very things that first allowed humans to develop the sense that something is indeed there.

We wonder why there are so many angry atheists who deny outright the existence of God using the same certainty fundamentalists do when they issue what they call apologetics. Simply put, because fundamentalism has caused the evolution of the human brain to turn backwards, to seek to close itself off from the possibility that we as humans do not know everything.

Engaging Christians from all stripes, learning about theology, science, and what it means to read a book without either accepting all of it or rejecting it out right propelled me along my way.

I had left Young Earth Creationism, King James Onlyism, Inerrancy-ism, and long left the idea that the dogmatic view of the Godhead was the key point in salvation. I had even broached the idea of the universal reconciliation. And I no longer hated the gays and a variety of other sinners. I still despise child molesters though with a hellish fervor.

But, see, this was on the inside. I could hide my theological movements better than my wife could hide her frustration with not cutting her hair — it was down to her ankles when she finally cut it off. However, we were both moving into the direction that it would make it impossible to return to The Church of Jesus Christ.

When she said what she said, I said what I said, I apologized, I begged her to give God another chance. See, I knew that Christianity was not supposed to be that way.

I asked her to allow us to visit a variety of churches to see if we could find a home, could find God in any of them, assuring her that the God of my aunts was not the God we had known. She allowed me.

I once was a community organizer, and during one pastoral visit, I had visited the pastor at Christ Church United Methodist Church. We could see the tower from our house. He was supportive of the issue I was trying to address and so I knew that he was okay at least on a few social issues. We attended the next morning, when none of the pastoral staff was there. What was there, however, was something that is beyond coincidence. It was a lecture on the prison ministry of the United Methodist Church. See, my wife wanted a place with a community outreach — not in evangelization, but in charity.

My son bounded out of service proclaiming how much he liked it. He wanted to go back. My oldest daughter didn't like the music, but she was happy as well. It was something different.

I knew what we would never be, not for "they are going to hell" reasons but for particular reasons. I didn't like the church government of the Baptists. Lutherans are okay, but Wesley is a better reformer. And, let me honest here, Christ Church United

Methodist Church. Do you see something there? The Church of Jesus Christ : Christ Church United Methodist.

The next Sunday was the last Sunday of the well-liked associate pastor. We felt a bit like guests at a funeral. We didn't get the inside jokes.

During that week, I had invited the pastor over so that we could talk. He came and we talked.

I sent him some follow up questions which he answered. The answer that perhaps resonated the most, the best, was that the United Methodist Church would not require us to think a certain way, only to think. Also, he had informed us that the new associate pastor would be a woman. I was not that advanced yet. I was worried about how I would react. Her first Sunday came and went and we continued to stay. My daughter has bloomed in this environment.

But during that first year or so, even after we had joined, even after we had joined a Sunday School class and participated in other activities, I was having a difficult time. See, I didn't leave The Church of Jesus Christ. I was kicked out. I was removed from everything I had known for 32 years. I was abandoned. And then, when I decided it was time to move on, I was worried — like that 8 year old child terrified that God would come back and I hadn't repented. This was the way I went to church every Sunday morning. Afraid. Petrified. But I survived.

I couldn't pray in the church for a very, very long time. See, we were taught that if we bowed our head down in any other church we were praying to that god, namely Satan. (By the way, we couldn't call those things churches. We called them dog houses, places of worship, dens of thieves, stuff like that)

I was surrounded by the worst sort of sinners — Protestants. And I knew, without a doubt, that if God returned, I would go to hell. I was an apostate. Crazy, I know, but that is how I felt. See, that Psychology of Religion bit is a funny thing.[18] I could not simply change my stars, so to speak. For 32 years, I had been taught that

---

18 Cooper, Joel M. *Cognitive Dissonance: 50 Years of a Classic Theory*. Sage Publications Ltd, 2007.

regardless of anything else, it was only The Church of Jesus Christ that held the truth, completely and without error. Therefore, all others were lost and going to hell. To leave The Church of Jesus Christ is to place oneself into the pit of Satan, ready only to be roasted alive.

Intellectually, I know that what I had done was right, but heart wise — my heart was still this bruised mess wondering if it would not be easier to die than to be a Methodist.

At one point, I nearly snapped. I cracked. My shell that once was destroyed, so I began to see a counselor. I needed the help. I needed something.

I was no longer one of the elite; nothing else was certain. The foundation that I had stood on for all of my life — the foundation that had brought me comfort time and time again, that foundation of black and white, either for or against, either holy or sinner was suddenly gone. With the Upper Big Branch tragedy, I was sent for an emotional loop that, to be honest, I have not yet fully recovered from. My inward man bore the scars. I was ripped away from everything that I had known, believed, and yes, loved. It was bloody and gooey, a cadaver really. What I didn't show people was the hurt uncertainty and doubt caused me. Whereas I had once relied upon my chosen status to get me through, I found that I was just like everyone else — a squirrel trying to get a nut. A child of God torn. I hated God. I hated God for allowing me not to know better. I hated God for allowing me to bring my wife and daughter, and then my son, into that way of life. I hated God for all of the things

---

Jeeves, Malcolm, and Warren S. Brown. Neuroscience, Psychology, and Religion: Illusions, Delusions, and Realities About Human Nature. Templeton Press, 2009.

PhD, Ralph W. Hood Jr, Peter C. Hill PhD, and Bernard Spilka PhD. *The Psychology of Religion, Fourth Edition: An Empirical Approach*. Fourth ed. The Guilford Press, 2009.

"The Science of Why We Don't Believe Science." *Mother Jones*, n.d. http://motherjones.com/politics/2011/03/denial-science-chris-mooney.

he had let go on under the name of Jesus Christ. I did. I swore at God. Job would blush at the things I said.

And I almost slipped into atheism, into agnosticism, into the abyss. There were days, there are days, I choose to believe rather than naturally believe. Does that make sense to you? See, some days, I hated God so much that I refused to believe in him. Some days, I pitied God and myself. Some days, I almost decided that God could take a flying leap because I was done with him. Some days, I trembled at the grace of God for finally opening my eyes to such a mess.

But I still felt like I was wrong, that I had sinned, by leaving. I still felt like I was going to collect God's wrath any day now because I had bad-mouthed the local church and disobeyed the pastor. Oh, and all the other stuff too. All of this came crashing down on me and I could not bear it. I could not bear the guilt and the shame of being a fundamentalist — or maybe, of having to be a Methodist. Like David, you see, I was forced to fight for the Philistine King against my own people. I was humiliated. What I had once taught, preached, and labored for was now my enemy. Or maybe, I was there enemy. This is not the best possible mental location to assume.

But eventually, through the help of the local church, through the help of my wife, of my Sunday School class, and of my counselor, most of those feelings began to subside. I was able to pray in Church. I was not ready to attack everyone around me. I was not hating too much. I was not as frustrated. I was not well, not healed, I should say.

Wait. That is not the entirety of how I made the transition. I sought help from one a counselor. Every other week, I would visit him and we would talk. He was accepting, but challenging. He did not dismiss what I was going through. At Christ Church, I joined a Sunday School class, a Disciple III class, and a MERGE class on Romans. This constant participation in the church helped me to keep from shrinking into the abyss that was as a black hole pulling me. The counselor talked me down from the ledge — I was ready to shuck it all. All. Let that sink in. All. Why should I continue in my same path if nothing was real, nothing is real, and God may in fact just be an angry sky dude? But having a Christian counselor is more than beneficial. Having a church family that appreciated just having us there, not because we were numbers, or young, or images, but because we were there built more confidence than words can express.

There was for a long while the temptation to return. Yes, I admit it. I wanted to return, not just in the Davidic way, but as a sinner begging forgiveness. Of course, I sometimes wanted to return as a ploy to stand up in church and confess my sins publicly. Did I miss this part? If you sinned against the pastor, even privately, you had to stand up in front of the church and state your sins while begging forgiveness. I thought that this may be a good way to bring it out in the open. See, none of the local church members were told much of anything, expect that other churches, like the one in Dyersburg, were dropping like flies because they were rebellious, liberal, pentecostal. But most days, I wanted simply go and sit and beg for acceptance. I am not the only one to feel this way. Indeed, my former stepmother still maintains that The Church of Jesus Christ is the only right Church in heaven or on earth. My little sister and her children, albeit on Christmas and Easter, still go there.

I know of numerous others who have left because they have seen the truth about this pastor or that pastor or because they have been brutally hurt or because they are sick and tired of the poisoness fruit around them. They still languish in exile, believing that they can only go to one place to worship God, as if we were in an ancient tribal religion where God dwells only in one finite location. This is, in part, is what drives me to write this chapter, to call them to go and find a place to worship God to discover the fruits of the spirit albeit even in a Methodist, Lutheran, or dare I say it, Roman Catholic Church.

The reason we find it so difficult to leave fundamentalism is because we have been brainwashed to see it as the only correct way, the only way to save our souls from hell. Not God, but fundamentalism. The reason we find it so difficult to accept the non-judgmental normative Christianity is because it seems like we are missing something. It is very much like the abused spouse who has confused love with violence, or the promiscuous person who has confused love with sex. Love without violence or love without sex does not feel like love. All of us who have experienced love without violence or love without letting ourselves be sexually used, cannot fully understand why people return to those situations, why they are drawn repeatedly back into the same lifestyle even when they know it to be harmful to them and those round them. It is because in our minds, we do not believe we deserve a love without violence, a love without being sexually used, a Christianity without authoritative judgment a God without hate.

I can safely same that I will never be like I once was — that self-assured, entitled, arrogant person who knew it all, was tough, not needy, and mean. That has been replaced with someone who is willing to learn and love. I'm not right about everything. Shoot, I may be wrong about everything, but I know this — that God is love.

What's life like now, you may ask? It's tough, but not as tough. I am able to talk more about my experiences and I am able to use the word cult a bit more freely. I am able to pray for those still in the cult and ask forgiveness for those that I have wrong in the past. I am sometimes unsure, sometimes worried, sometimes needy, sometimes stronger, sometimes not. But, I am still growing. We attend a United Methodist Church where just last week I gave my first sermon. It was written. No jumping, no shouting. It was for a class. A seminary class.

I graduated seminary in 2012 and then, to doctoral work.

The danger of leaving fundamentalism is deeply emotional, spiritual, and psychological. I have shared some of my struggle with you. It was difficult. I didn't like my wife and my children. On that Saturday of our break-through, I knew that the legalistic structures would not stay. Yet, I had always been told that the woman who cuts her hair or wear pants were little more than whores. Okay, they were whores, prostitutes, sex-fiends. They were sluts, just wanted to show their bodies off. Fathers who let their daughters do these things were selling them off the sex trade. Every new change became a hurdle. My wife worked with me through this. She didn't cut her hair for a very long time. I couldn't participate. I sat outside and waited. When my daughter wanted to wear pants to school instead of skirts, I nearly died. Intellectually, I was okay with it, but emotionally, I was tied to the notion that the woman, any woman, had to dress a certain way. These changes were difficult to accept. When I decided to wear shorts for the first time in eight years, I did so only in the house, but would change to go and check the mail. I was afraid of anyone seeing us dressed this certain way.

My faith has grown considerably. I do not know who said it, but my personal motto is "faith needs doubt like children need love." Doubt is the water of our faith. If we can explore what it means to challenge God, to doubt God, then we can know what it means to rely upon him, to have faith in him. Would I say I was more spiritual? Yes, yes I would. I would say a few other things, but honestly, isn't this chapter long enough?

There is a danger in moving away from fundamentalism. In the inerrancy debate, you will often hear that if one part of the Bible is not true, then none of it is. Usually, this is in reference to the Young Earth Creationist belief. When I first realized that there were contradictions in the text, it did not worry me so much. But I know others who spend every waking hour attempting to pick a part Scripture to show the contradiction. This person tells me two things. First, he has not really left his belief in the inerrant word of God. See, he is still arguing with it. Second, this person doesn't get the point of Scripture. Scripture is not our constitution. It is the deposit of the revelation of God to his people. It is not revelation. If it was revelation, then there would be some serious heretical problems with Scripture. Remember, Tradition comes first.

Tradition regarding who God is, what his prophets did, and what the people should do came long before the written word. The canon — the collection of books in your bible — came long after the writings were written down and circulated. Once I realized how important a role Tradition played, I was able to rely more fully on the Christians that had come before me for 2000 years. Scripture is still first and foremost in my Christian life. It is the thing I wrestle with daily. Yes, as an academic, I study it; but as a Christian, I believe it. I bill myself as a conservative in this regard, because for Christians, Scripture is still supposed to matter. I do not believe every common interpretation but I attempt to get back to the original meaning. For many, this makes me a liberal. For instance, I believe in Genesis 1 but I do not believe it speaks about a 6000 year old earth. So, I use Scripture first, Tradition second, and Reason third.

What of Scripture? I have yet to find a license to the deny the authority of Scripture; however, I no longer believe that Scripture is to be read like a post-Enlightenment IKEA technical manual. I challenge interpretations, but I cannot ignore the precepts of Scripture. Think not that because I accept a scientific view of the origins (the how) of the universe that I have suddenly lost the accurate depiction of the origins (the why) of the universe as provided by Genesis 1 and the origins of the covenant as provided by Genesis 2-3.[19] Nor have I turned my back on Romans 1.28-32, but I just know a more faithful way of reading those verses.[20] Likewise, when

---

19 Brettler, Marc Zvi, Peter Enns, and Daniel J. Harrington. *The Bible and the Believer: How to Read the Bible Critically and Religiously.* Oxford University Press, USA, 2012.

Byas, Jared, and Peter Enns. *Genesis for Normal People (Study Guide Edition): A Guide to the Most Controversial, Misunderstood, and Abused Book of the Bible.* Patheos Press, 2012.

Enns, Peter. Evolution of Adam, The: What the Bible Does and Doesn't Say About Human Origins. Brazos Press, 2012.

————. *Inspiration and Incarnation: Evangelicals and the Problem of the Old Testament.* annotated ed. Baker Academic, 2005.

20 Watts, Joel L. "But, Romans 1.26-27 Isn't About Creation or Homosexuality...." *Unsettled Christianity*, n.d. http://unsettledchristianity.com/2012/05/but-romans-1-26-27-isnt-about-creation-or-homosexuality/.

I read Paul's first letter to the church at Corinth, I can now better understand the rhetorical questions Paul is answering, including his disdain of the mistreatment of women. And now, Paul is not keen on women acting subservient to men or keeping their hair uncut. I do not have it right, but I believe we come close to it when we remember the role Scripture is supposed to play in the Church.[21]

I struggled with the Trinity for a very long time after I left. As a matter of fact, one of the questions asked to the pastor was whether or not I had to believe in the Trinity. We were taught that the Trinity is the tool of the devil.[22] Just a few weeks before we decided to seek fellowship elsewhere, my wife had asked me about the Trinity — if I still believed the same way, if it was still important. Yes, I lied. It was. But it wasn't. Yes, I bow to the Tradition of the Church, and yes, I in my own way believe in the Trinity, more so than the false notion that it was the Father who died on the Cross. But now, it is not so important to me. As a Christian, you have to have several important tenets to your view of the Godhead. First, Christ is divine. Second, Christ is not an angel or other divine

---

―――. "Paul's Use of Prosopopoeia in His Epistle to the Romans." *Unsettled Christianity*, n.d. http://unsettledchristianity.com/2010/01/pauls-use-of-prosopopoeia-in-his-epistle-to-the-romans/.

―――. "Romans 6-8, Contra Stowers." *Unsettled Christianity*, n.d. http://unsettledchristianity.com/2011/12/romans-6-8-contra-stowers/.

―――. "Stowers, Protreptic Rhetoric and Romans." *Unsettled Christianity*, n.d. http://unsettledchristianity.com/2011/11/stowers-pro-trepic-rhetoric-and-romans/.

―――. "Too Brief of an Exegesis on Romans 8.1-17." *Unsettled Christianity*, n.d. http://unsettledchristianity.com/2011/11/too-brief-of-an-exegesis-on-romans-8-1-17/.

21   Wright, N. T. *Scripture and the Authority of God: How to Read the Bible Today.* HarperOne, 2011.

22   For a roundly debunked book that is as important to Oneness Christians as *Trial of Blood* is to Landmark Baptists, see: Hislop, Alexander, and Alexander Hislop. *The Two Babylons.* 4th ed. Chick Pub, 1998.

figure. He is divine in the same way the Father is.[23] For me, again, I bow to the Tradition of the Church found in the earliest creeds, namely the Apostles'.[24] Here, I stand, and here I can go no further.

What about the move of the Spirit, the so-called Pentecostal fire. To be honest, the Wesleyans had it first. I have felt the Spirit a time or two or three in the United Methodist Church and I cannot tell you how important this was to me — how comforting to me this was. Do I speak in tongues? No. Do I raise my hands? No. Do I feel all tickle-y and the such? Yes. I do not doubt too much the experiences I had in the previous place. I believe that there are always psychological elements to religion that can produce what is nothing more than a bit of mass hysteria. I also believe that there are genuine moments of divine inspiration upon a person. I cannot judge others, but only my own experience here. Do I discount the "spiritual experiences?" No, I can't. There are issues with them, of course.[25] Anthropologists may note the idea of mob rule (see most of the work by René Girard) and how we are influenced by our surroundings and the expectation of those surroundings. Perhaps this drives the wild, uncontrollable ecstatic utterances found in the pentecostal and charismatic churches — not them only, but more

---

23 Athanasius, Saint. *On the Incarnation*. Empire Books, 2012.

24 González, Justo L. *The Apostles' Creed for Today*. annotated ed. Westminster John Knox Press, 2007.

Johnson, Luke Timothy. *The Creed: What Christians Believe and Why It Matters*. Image, 2004.

McGrath, Alister. *"I Believe": Exploring the Apostles' Creed*. IVP Books, 1998.

Packer, J. I. *Affirming the Apostles' Creed*. Crossway, 2008.

Pannenberg, Wolfhart. *The Apostles' Creed in the Light of Today's Questions*. New ed. SCM Press, 2011.

25 Carey, Benedict. "A Neuroscientific Look at Speaking in Tongues." *The New York Times*, November 7, 2006, sec. Health. http://www.nytimes.com/2006/11/07/health/07brain.html.

Rice, John R. *The Charismatic Movement*. Sword of the Lord, 2000.

"Speaking in Tongues." *About.com Christianity*, n.d. http://christianity.about.com/od/glossary/g/speakingtongues.htm.

primitive religions as well. This is one of the main pitfalls of those making the transition — to not discount the previous experiences, but to categorize them as a progression.

What about modesty and the such? We used to believe that the person was to be at all times modest, especially the woman. Brenda, the pastor's wife at Ohley believed that a woman could not show elbows. They were too provocative. No open toed shows. A woman's hair was not to be cut. No beards for either the woman or man. Kidding. Women could grow beards. They couldn't wear make-up or anything. Jewelry was limited to a wedding ring and maybe a watch. Nothing flashy. Well, the men could. The preachers started to wear some of the most distasteful suits. Purple zoot suits and worse.[26] Today, we are careful about the way our children dress but mindful of their personalities. We encourage them to dress modest, but only in the fact that they respect themselves.

Do we drink? Some. Smoke? No. I also don't curse. Nothing wrong with that, but I don't do it. I don't judge others as well.

I've spoken about exclusion, inclusion, and the ecumenical spirit. Christianity, in my opinion is the only way God has provided for us. Nothing else. Unfortunately, we do not really explore what that means. I detest denominations still, but for a different reason. I view Christianity through the lens of John 17. One of the most detrimental aspects of fundamentalism is the avenue of exclusion. More often than not, fundamentalists are defined by their go it alone attitude wherein they disavow other Christian denominations. Catholics are usually considered agents of Satan, infecting us all. You need look no further than the Jack Chick tracts handed out every now and then by well-meaning souls. The higher the church, the more likely one is too lost to be saved. There is no ecumenical spirit at work among the fundamentalist churches because such a move is the very definition of their eschatological fear of a one

---

26 Watts, Joel L. "Proud as Peacocks: The Hypocrisy of the Holiness Movement." *Unsettled Christianity*, n.d. http://unsettledchristianity. com/2009/04/proud-as-peacocks-the-hypocrisy-of-the-holiness-movement/.

world government and a one world church. They are adamant that they along hold the proper keys to salvation and interpretation. They need no one else. As mentioned above, had The Church of Jesus Christ engaged in an ecumenical dialogue, it is possible that many of their abuses could have been curtailed. This is not likely to change for The Church of Jesus Christ or the other fundamentalist sects surviving today, especially those who view the King James as the only bible.

I think that one of the larger questions I've been asked is if I still believe in sin. I do. I believe that sin is a darkness, a sickness, that plagues humankind. I do not believe, however, I it is summed up in abortion, homosexuality, and being Catholic. Indeed, in many ways the arrogance of fundamentalism trumps the sins of the world. We proclaim to know the truth, to have the truth, and yet, our truth enslaves. I think sin is bigger than what I once thought it was — harsher, more frightening. Sin is the abuse of others in the name of God; sin is the denial of who we are as God's creation. Yes, I believe in Sin and the death it causes, but now I have a pretty good idea about the limitations of Sin as well.

And what of my faith? My faith has grown considerably. I have experienced some pretty dark times in the transition and I feel confident that these times are best explained by neuroscience and psychology rather than the rumors passed around about me that I was in fact demon possessed. The fundamentalist, I must charge, has no real faith. Faith is the expectation of things we have yet to see. It does not involve fear. The fear of God, as Tyndale translated it, is more about reverence than fear. What the fundamentalist has is just this, fear and the need to know everything. The fundamentalist lives in a black and white world where it is an either/or proposition, usually proposed by themselves in order to shield any moment of doubt in their minds. This, my friends, is not faith. This is fear. A fundamentalist has no god but his own fear. This is why so many moved into a militant atheism. They simply replaced one epistemological certainty with another.

Faith must be equal parts expectation and doubt. It must include questions and the courage to ask them. Some of you will point to Job. I would question you as to if you have actually read it. YHWH and one of his angels made a bet that the angel could in fact do everything possible to the man of God, except take his life. This is YHWH, the one we love and serve and he is the one who bet a man's life for a point of pride. Whereas we are mislead to read Job as a man about patience, instead, you must read the Job as a book that is a question in of itself. Is it right to question God when your life falls a part? Yes, it is. Question God. Doubt God. Remember, we know the full story; Job does not. We know about the bet.

The fundamentalist is one who lives in a world that is so fragile that any hint of change threatens it. I speak here from experience. I know what it is like to fear science, to fear breakthroughs in technology, in scholarship. Yet, all truth is God's truth, all change is God's change. In John 16, Christ promises us the Spirit to lead us into all truth. Truth is by its very nature a changing substance. When Truth enters our perception, we must change to accept it. Here also is a hint in Scripture that Scripture does not hold the entire revelation of God. If this is the case, then we must understand that the Spirit will work to bring about the entirety of God's truth through progressive revelation, through science, through you. I do not mean here to say that truth will change or that we must change our beliefs about God to match science. But we can accept science, change, because God has given us two books and they inform one another. Do not be afraid of change because if God is who we believe he is, then all truth will point to him. If we are challenged, this does not mean God is challenged. Change.

I have had no contact with anyone from The Church of Jesus Christ. I can say this honestly although I have met at least one who finally divorced them as well. I have no desire to meet with them, to break bread with them. There is no healing the rift, so to speak. There is no going our own separate ways. I do not judge them, but I pity them. I know the prison they are in and I know who controls the shadows on their cell wall. I love them on most days, but I never like them. Yes, perhaps some of this is pride, but as you can tell, it is difficult to one day realize the people that you had so much faith in, so much love and respect for, are the very ones causing you so much pain. There are other stories to be told, not just about this group but about other groups. I know of families torn a part, of children scarred by their parents' involvement in The Church of Jesus Christ. Yes, there are come that have put away drugs and alcohol, but I fully suspect that instead of getting past their addiction, they have simply changed their addiction.[27] I do not fault them for that. And perhaps that is why transitions are so fearful, because you fear becoming the person you think you have repressed.

If this is your fear, that person remains. This is not what Scripture teaches.

The transition is difficult although it is getting better. This is not the end of my journey, to be sure; however, I am in a much better place. I can stand now and still feel ashamed of the former life in fundamentalism and I can know full-well how Paul felt when he wrote Galatians, but I have accepted that feeling of shame as something beneficial. It is like Paul's blindness in the same letter. It is a mark one wears proudly to display the Grace of God that much more fully. This grace of God I can see stretching back across my life. Yes, I was mean to my mother. I've been mean to a lot of people. I've judged a lot of people. I've cursed a lot of people. I have preached sermons, I have turned the blind eye. I have excluded people because they were apostates. I have urged for a stricter association for The Church of Jesus Christ, to measure up to a stricter view of Scripture.

I have hated Catholics and Protestants alike. I have marched across time to laugh at the theologies of Wesley, Calvin, and Luther who could only still be children of a whore. I have watched the conspiracy theories develop with the Jesuits and that really good

27 Dunnington, Kent. *Addiction and Virtue: Beyond the Models of Disease and Choice*. IVP Academic, 2011.

one about how the Catholic Church started Islam. I have watched how the Trinity was held up and I laugh at it, declaring it a mark no better than John's 666. And I have stood at the foot of the cross, spear in hand.

Now, I live in a world of gray; but the certainty of God is there, it's just that I have to seek him to know him. I hear his voice. I do not fear him. I love him. I am often times still unsteady, but I look at my family and I see real Christian growth. I look at me and I hope for the same. I know Jesus better now. It is not just ME and Jesus. But because of the forgiveness of sins, I stand in the communion of saints, the holy catholic Church, in the Holy Ghost ready to be judged when Jesus comes for the live and the dead, comes from the right hand of God where he ascended to after he was resurrected from the death Pilate gave to him — he who was born of a virgin by conception of the Holy Spirit; he is the only begotten Son, our Lord, the only Son of the one who made the heavens and earth, is still almighty, God the Father.

You have read my story long enough to pick up some of the inherent dangers of a fundamentalistic mindset, but I want to briefly reiterate them. Fundamentalism is defined by the approach to any topic that prevents challenges. This is why I can use fundamentalist as a pejorative for liberals as well. A fundamentalistic belief system will refuse to all you to challenge "known facts." It often relies on its own traditions while eschewing legitimate tradition as somehow corrupt. This is about control. The control exhibited in fundamentalism promises acceptance if you just believe this. It is about orthodoxy, then, but only the group in charge decides the orthodoxy. You must think this way find acceptance. This creates spiritual abuse through manipulation of emotions and thoughts. It is not the fear of hell that drives you any longer; it is the fear that your congregational brothers and sisters will not accept you. That is a particular worse form of hell, something even Dante could not have imagined.

Spiritual abuse leads all sorts of abuse. This is why we see those who are "no longer in church" acting in such a way as to showcase this fact but still uttering the idea that there is only one right place to go. This is a prison, a box, a method of control. Fundamentalism will allow you to act out, to sin, to go wild, but it demands that you return to it because it alone will absolve you of your sins, or those things they tell you are sins. Let me be a bit clearer for a moment. A fundamentalist will die a well-known sinner rather than seek forgiveness from God in a church they consider "other." This is why I returned so often, because regardless of how I was treated, or what had happened in the meantime, I was convinced that The Church of Jesus Christ alone was the only place I could be pardoned of my transgressions. I was controlled, even when I thought I was free. Perhaps this is a bit of a Pavlovian existence.

Fundamentalism will lead you to abuse not just yourself as described above, but so too others. You will need to shun your friends and family, even in subtle ways. You will need to believe that regardless of their faith, it is counterfeit. This too is a method of control, so that you will see them with nothing but pity, as if their happiness is a blinding spell by Satan. You will turn on your immediate family as well. They are in it with you and provide you, especially if you are a male, with the image needed to be presentable. Your children will need to act a certain way — usually as lifeless dolls ready to be placed on this altar or in that picture to showcase just how godly of a family you are. If they do not listen, you are expected to maintain control and order. If they do shun your way of life, they are to be shunned, if not publicly, then privately through testimonies given in church, or subtle prayer requests designed to show everyone just how much better you are than your family. If you are a male, this is much worse. Your wife is your key into the club, so to speak. She had best be the demure little woman, homemaker, caretaker, and servant. If she has a question, you had best stop this train of thought soon enough. If she wants to leave the church, you will know what this means for you, that you will be the outcast, the pitied, the one who could not control his family — like God intended, of course.

The ultimate danger of fundamentalism is simply this: there is no god. The god many fundamentalists make does not exist. God, if they do intend to worship him, is hidden behind control, anger, wrath, vengefulness. God is only accessible through perfect obedience to unquestionable doctrines. God is the sole intellectual property of the sect leadership, usually the pastor and whatever tradition he wishes to maintain. God is not good. God is not love. God is waiting to throw you into hell. Question Scripture in some way? Doctrine? Statements by the pastor? This all leads to the "overthrowing of the Lordship of Christ," a favorite statement by fearful fundamentalists who deny the basic human dignity of questioning. Questioning leaders to answers — silence is an answer in of itself. Answers leader to knowledge. Knowledge leads to a lack of certainty. A lack of certainty leaders to real faith. Real faith leads to the end of fundamentalism.

Where will I go from here? No doubt, I will continue to stand firm in my faith; however, the firmness of mind and security is something that may never really be recovered. I still seek help from friends, counselors and my wife. I still have this guilt of that I did to others in the name of Jesus Christ. There is one guy, at the funeral of a woman he called mother, and I refused to shake his hand or acknowledge him in any way because, well, he had left the Church. Or the guilt I owe to my own family — my wife and my daughter. After all, I brought them there and manipulated my wife into staying for a long time. Now, I will maintain that I was not just like them — after all, I left. Had I been completely aligned, I would never have left, never challenged them on any thing. Yet, I did, often. But, I passed on the spiritual abuse that was handed down to me. If I was forced to act a part, I made sure she acted a part. If I was forced to keep quiet and never ask question, well, she had best not ask one either. The manipulation, the control, the abuse I was handed I passed on. Realizing my active part in this is only the beginning of another leg of the journey. I have overcome much of my anger at the spiritual abuse handed down, but the guilt I have for the way I treated others, that is not likely to subside anytime soon. So, I have developed this sort of penance — small acts towards forgiveness by others and to myself — to keep myself reminded but in a way to liberate myself as well. Maybe this is not the best Protestant way of doing things, but it is my way.

When you realize the role you play in perpetrating spiritual abuse — either by shunning questions, by manipulation of others, or even by preaching that regardless of the blood of Christ, everyone else but your group would bust hell wide open — then you take stock of your life, your spirituality, your position before God. I did not kill as Paul did, but I would argue with him over which one of us persecuted the Church of God more. I was a Christian, I thought, making the narrow path narrower. I was going to heaven and, frankly, needed no one else to go. God was an angry, wrathful being — controlling, much like my earthly father, abusive. Whereas my earthly father was physically abusive, my heavenly father was himself spiritually abusive. And I was his son, to carry out this abuse, or rather this Gospel, on earth. Gospel. The Good News. I, we, did not preach a good news. We preached death and destruction. We preached a god who I know longer believe in.

Often times, fundamentalists will decry the so-called slippery slope. Yes, I stopped believing in the King James. I started carrying with me the New Living Translation, the Study Bible version due to having received it as a review copy from Tyndale. I started to read books like John Walton's *The Lost World of Genesis One* (Intervarsity Press, 2009) and discovered that there was a deeply theological way of looking at Scripture, rather than examining it as a cold, metallic version of an IKEA manual. I started to reading the Church Fathers, to listen to the words of the Creeds, to hear a God who was speaking to the Church. I found books by N.T. Wright and others, theologians who served in academia. They didn't believe like I did, but then again, I didn't believe like I did. No, I started to hear a God who was alive and well, and calling. This God was calling and not shunning, calling everyone to love and to be loved. I found God in Scripture, in Knowledge, in Science, in Nature, in love.

I carry my guilt and shame with me, and there were more days that I desire nothing more than to end it all. Today, I have the baggage stored properly, or more properly. I doubt myself more than I ever did, but I know what humility, what humiliation is. I doubt God, but then again, this makes reading the Book of Job a lot more interesting. I love. I fear. I rejoice. I explore. But I do not hate.

I do understand Galatians a bit better though…

I will continue to grow in God, to explore new facets of the Christian faith. I'll explore panetheism, academia, and Christian mysticism. I'll explore the love of God, the certainty of God — but never the certainty of me, the hatred of them. I will continue to seek to help those who are coming from fundamentalism. I might not get everything right, but I will try. I will continue the long, dark night of the soul, the ascension to God, the theosis.

16

You Don't Have to Go It Alone

Ric Hardison

I haven't experienced it directly myself. But vicariously, I have learned the extent to which those living in the realm of fundamentalism are under extreme control of other humans. But it is nearly impossible for the subjects of fundamentalism to see it that it way. That's because the tenets and directives are presented as scripturally based. Who can argue with God and His Holy Word? What is one to do when suspicions begin to arise that something is just not right?

At the risk of making fundamentalism (and other highly controlling Christian groups) sound like a disease, an antidote must be found. For it to be acceptable, the antidote must itself rest securely upon scripture. But the antidote must be more than an intellectual acceptance of a scriptural truth. It must also be a matter of heart and feelings. I know of no better starting point than the statement: "You have no idea how much God loves you." If you are proceeding through the transition out of fundamentalism, you can stand freely and joyously on this foundation in face of all intellectual confusion and emotional upheaval.

In fundamentalism control, one is constantly being judged. In God's love, acceptance is available—and the acceptance is not withdrawn if you make mistakes or bad choices. The acceptance is unconditional, flowing from a heavenly Father who, while challenging us to righteousness and Christ-likeness, understands our human frailty. This was seen when he sent His Son to live among us as the perfect blend of grace and truth (John 1:14). In this, the truth of God's mandates and limitations—which are the hallmark of fundamentalism—is tempered with His grace—which is lacking in fundamentalism.

Questions keep coming: How is one who is considering a transition out of any strict Christian control able to be confident that God is any more gracious than his/her religious leaders? By experiencing it from another person. A basic tenet of human mental health is that any wounding at the hands of a person is best healed at the hands of a different person. So if you are on, on near, a journey out of fundamentalism, may I make a simple recommendation? Find a companion for your journey.

As a professional Christian counselor, I have found joy in accompanying more than one person as they try to make sense of the complex thoughts and feelings that come with the transition we are considering. But your companion need not be a professional. A pastor, good friend or any other trusted mentor will do. What you will need has more to do with attitude than aptitude. Look for someone who:

- accepts a wide range of spiritual behavior—within scriptural limits
- is comfortable with confusion and cyclical rather than linear progress
- provides a safe place for the expression of fear, sadness, anger and other troubling thoughts and feelings

Please don't give up on all humans. You are wise to be cautious and self protective. You have the right to proceed at your own pace. You have the right to test us before opening up.

Most of all, please don't give up on God.

CONCLUSION

TRAVIS MILAM

What is it about religion that makes many of us fearful? The essays here were written by those who believe their stories need to be told. They believe that the faith they now possess is all the more precious to them because of the fear they lived and endured for so long. They believe that if one person is given hope in their words, then they have made a difference.

Each of the essays included here are by those who retained faith even after their struggle with their fear. The saddest statement is that there are many who suffered the same fears, suffered the same problems with what was taught in their churches and turned away from their faith. They said that if this is what God is like they want nothing to do with Him. These essays demonstrate that one can wrestle with the issues that have come with the fear and overcome. It is not easy, but it can be done.

Jesus never motivated anyone to follow him by using fear. He had kind words for those who came with questions, but was a tad less kind to those who caused someone to stumble or added burdens. He was gentle and understanding using love and compassion. The times there was fear, Jesus calmed those fears. Would Jesus want us to follow him if it were out of fear? I believe we know the answer to that question.

One may not call it fear. It could be legalism, it could be fundamentalism, could be whatever it was called. The single factor that ties them all together is fear. Fear of the unknown, fear of rejection, fear of disappointing God. The list goes on and on.

Thank God that we can be released from that fear. We can come to a faith where we see who we are in Him and that He loves us not for what we do, but for who we follow. Each person here realized that. May we all come to see that the journey from fear to faith starts with a single step, and that the journey is never made by only one, but by many.

ALSO FROM ENERGION PUBLICATIONS

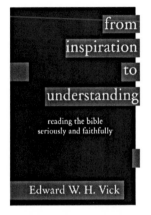

Professor Vick's approach to the Bible is informed, clear, and immensely helpful. If we view the Scriptures as the means by which God is revealed to the community of faith, he argues, we can account for the Bible's authority, without trying to "prove" it. And on this basis, we can appreciate the complex history and varied contents of the Bible, while avoiding the pitfalls that surround mistaken views of "biblical inspiration."

Richard Rice
Professor of Religion
Loma Linda University

Weiss is retired now, but still actively involved in a Spanish Seventh-Day Adventist congregation local to him. How is this possible? Because he long ago, maybe with the help of Bultmann and later his fellow colleagues, realized that one could continue to question and advocate for a richer faith through historical criticism and still find his way in a congregation of the faithful.

Joel Watts
unsettledchristianity.com

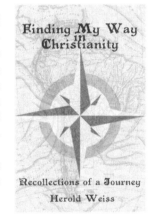

God's command is to question the true source, and Henry provides us with five scriptural instructions for proper discernment. More than this, Henry believes we have every right to question the Bible's authority as well. Can we trust the development of the canon (those books considered "inspired" and thus selected for our Bible)? Can we read every word in the Bible as God-breathed? As inerrant?

The Dubious Disciple

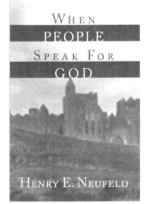

MORE FROM ENERGION PUBLICATIONS

Personal Study

Finding My Way in Christianity	Herold Weiss	$16.99
Holy Smoke! Unholy Fire	Bob McKibben	$14.99
The Jesus Paradigm	David Alan Black	$17.99
When People Speak for God	Henry Neufeld	$17.99
The Sacred Journey	Chris Surber	$11.99

Christian Living

Faith in the Public Square	Robert D. Cornwall	$16.99
Grief: Finding the Candle of Light	Jody Neufeld	$8.99
Crossing the Street	Robert LaRochelle	$16.99

Bible Study

Learning and Living Scripture	Lentz/Neufeld	$12.99
From Inspiration to Understanding	Edward W. H. Vick	$24.99
Philippians: A Participatory Study Guide	Bruce Epperly	$9.99
Ephesians: A Participatory Study Guide	Robert D. Cornwall	$9.99

Theology

Creation in Scripture	Herold Weiss	$12.99
Creation: the Christian Doctrine	Edward W. H. Vick	$12.99
The Politics of Witness	Allan R. Bevere	$9.99
Ultimate Allegiance	Robert D. Cornwall	$9.99
History and Christian Faith	Edward W. H. Vick	$9.99
The Church Under the Cross	William Powell Tuck	$11.99
The Journey to the Undiscovered Country	William Powell Tuck	$9.99
Eschatology: A Participatory Study Guide	Edward W. H. Vick	$9.99

Ministry

Clergy Table Talk	Kent Ira Groff	$9.99
Wind and Whirlwind	David Moffett-Moore	$9.99
Out of This World	Darren McClellan	$24.99

Generous Quantity Discounts Available
Dealer Inquiries Welcome
Energion Publications — P.O. Box 841
Gonzalez, FL_ 32560
Website: http://energionpubs.com
Phone: (850) 525-3916

* Full of typos. Needs proofreading
* Feminist. Includes stories from female pastors. Editor is pro.
* Article of KJVO is good, but descends into apparent conspiracy theorist ideas re: "The powers that be" & ESV onlyism, which I found odd & a little out of place. It had a "fundamentalist" ring to its logic.
* Some of the stories are patchy & sketchy, leaving out what are, to me, important connecting factors. Perhaps a necessary consequence of the book's format, but leaves one asking "why?"

Lightning Source UK Ltd.
Milton Keynes UK
UKOW042138030613

211702UK00006B/828/P